SCIENCE FOR EXCELLENCE

LEVEL 3

biological science

Scottish Schools Science Group

Series Editors:
Nicky Souter, Paul Chambers and Stephen Jeffrey

Authors:
Nicky Souter, Pat Carney, Eileen McClure,
Karen Parker and Robert Rowney

DYNAMIC LEARNING

HODDER GIBSON

The front cover shows a computer-generated artwork of yeast cells. Yeast cells are single-cell fungi. Some yeasts have industrial uses, for example in brewing and baking.

Although every effort has been made to ensure that website addresses are correct at time of going to press, Hodder Gibson cannot be held responsible for the content of any website mentioned in this book. It is sometimes possible to find a relocated web page by typing in the address of the home page for a website in the URL window of your browser.

Hachette UK's policy is to use papers that are natural, renewable and recyclable products and made from wood grown in sustainable forests. The logging and manufacturing processes are expected to conform to the environmental regulations of the country of origin.

Whilst every effort has been made to check the instructions of practical work in this book, it is still the duty and legal obligation of schools to carry out their own risk assessment.

Orders: please contact Bookpoint Ltd, 130 Milton Park, Abingdon, Oxon OX14 4SB. Telephone: (44) 01235 827720. Fax: (44) 01235 400454. Lines are open 9.00–5.00, Monday to Saturday, with a 24-hour message answering service. Visit our website at www.hoddereducation.co.uk. Hodder Gibson can be contacted direct on: Tel: 0141 848 1609; Fax: 0141 889 6315; email: hoddergibson@hodder.co.uk

© Scottish Schools Science Group 2010
First published in 2010 by
Hodder Gibson, an imprint of Hodder Education,
An Hachette UK Company
2a Christie Street
Paisley PA1 1NB

Impression number   5 4 3 2
Year   2013

Cover photo DAVID MACK/SCIENCE PHOTO LIBRARY
Illustrations by Emma Golley at Redmoor Design, Tony Wilkins, and DC Graphic Design Limited, Swanley, Kent
Typeset in Minion 12/15pt by DC Graphic Design Limited, Swanley, Kent
Printed in Dubai

A catalogue record for this title is available from the British Library

ISBN: 978 1444 110 784

Contents

Introduction

The first three Science for Excellence titles support learning at the Level Three outcomes of Curriculum for Excellence (CfE). This title focuses on Biological Systems and draws from the other organisers. It attempts to form a coherent link between the second and third level outcomes. It also makes frequent links to the key concepts identified in Curriculum for Excellence in that the chapters' contents cross into the organisers Forces, Electricity and Waves, Planet Earth, Materials and Topical Science.

Where appropriate, the Science for Excellence titles use familiar content and approaches while also embracing the principles of Curriculum for Excellence. The books also attempt to take the topics through to a natural conclusion and to provide, where appropriate, more demanding contexts for pupils.

Modern applications feature prominently throughout each chapter. The book provides many real life examples and applications of the principles which create opportunities for pupils to learn and appreciate the factors which led to the scientific discoveries, while also being aware of the implications of scientific advances and their impact on society and the environment. It is hoped that extending the scope of the content beyond the traditional 'biology' boundaries will develop a more rounded appreciation of science and society and will lead to greater motivation and a deeper understanding of the issues.

Some of the activities in the book involve experiments. These should only be attempted under the instruction of the Science Teacher and in accordance with the appropriate safety guidelines. Questions and activities are designed to examine and extend the content of the chapters. Skills in literacy and numeracy as well as an awareness of the importance of health and wellbeing will be developed through these exercises – look out for the icons shown at the end of this introduction. Some chapters allow for numerical and graphical activities while others seek to reinforce the scientific principles contained in the main text. Curriculum for Excellence encourages learners to become active participants and the Active Learning activities in this Science for Excellence series encourage open-ended and pupil investigation activities as well as individual and group project and research work where learners are asked to make informed decisions on scientific advances which may have ethical or societal implications. Tasks are designed around the 'broad features of assessment in science'.

By engaging in the activities and tasks pupils will show features of the skills sought in the 'principles and practice' documentation. Pupils will have the opportunity to demonstrate work that will allow teachers to assess:

- How well do they contribute to investigations and experiments?

- Are they developing the capacity to engage with and complete tasks and assignments?

- To what extent do they recognise the impact the sciences make on their lives, on the lives of others, on the environment and on society?

The principles and practices outlined in Curriculum for Excellence have been adopted throughout Science for Excellence. The series is designed to be used in conjunction with schemes of work which reflect learning and teaching approaches which are most applicable to the sciences. The chapters provide opportunities for scientific enquiry and examples of scientific scenarios where pupils can, for example, link variables to determine relationships, improve their scientific thinking or make informed judgements on the basis of scientific principles.

Scientifically Literate Citizens

The use of real data and experimental-type situations will help to develop scientific attitudes. Pupils will be able to look at the data critically and make informed judgements on the basis of what is in front of them. Additionally, they will be critical of broad or bold claims and be able to analyse the science as well as the implications of such claims. Ultimately, the significant challenge for CfE is that it changes pupils' attitudes to science and makes them more able to engage positively in issues that will affect them; that they are able to understand the scientific challenges and issues facing them and respond in a critical and informed manner.

CfE documentation states:

Learning in the sciences will enable me to:

- develop curiosity and understanding of the environment and my place in the living, material and physical world

- demonstrate a secure knowledge and understanding of the big ideas and concepts of the sciences

- develop skills for learning, life and work

- develop the skills of scientific inquiry and investigation using practical techniques

- develop skills in the accurate use of scientific language, formulae and equations

- apply safety measures and take necessary actions to control risk and hazards

- recognise the impact the sciences make on my life, the lives of others, the environment and on society

- recognise the role of creativity and inventiveness in the development of the sciences

- develop an understanding of the Earth's resources and the need for responsible use of them

- express opinions and make decisions on social, moral, ethical, economic and environmental issues based upon sound understanding

- develop as a scientifically-literate citizen with a lifelong interest in the sciences

- establish the foundation for more advanced learning and future careers in the sciences and the technologies.

 Literacy

 Numeracy

 Health and Wellbeing

PLANET EARTH
Biodiversity and Interdependence

Where are the living things?

Level 2 — What came before?

 SCN 2-01a

I can identify and classify examples of living things, past and present, to help me appreciate their diversity. I can relate physical and behavioural characteristics to their survival or extinction.

 SCN 2-17a

Having explored the substances that make up Earth's surface, I can compare some of their characteristics and uses.

Level 3 — What is this chapter about?

 SCN 3-01a

I can sample and identify living things from different habitats to compare their biodiversity and can suggest reasons for their distribution.

 SCN 3-17a

Through evaluation of a range of data, I can describe the formation, characteristics, and uses of soils, minerals, and basic types of rocks.

Where are the living things?

Techniques for collecting living things

The simplest thing you can do is to carefully pick up a living thing, observe it closely, record what it looks like, and return it to where it came from.

Looking closely

Try making and recording as many observations as possible when you look at something new so that you will be able to identify it in the future. Look at this plant, its flowers and its leaves.

Where did it come from? What are the conditions like where it lives? Describe its shape, size, colour, and texture (how it feels). Does it smell or have a taste?

!TAKE CARE if you do this – it might be poisonous!

Looking even more closely

When you use a hand lens you will be able to see things in even more detail. Here is how to use it properly and get the best results.

Hold the lens close to your eye, in the same position as a spectacles lens. Bring the object close to your eye.

Sampling land animals

Signs

Scientists often use the signs that have been left behind by animals.

These paw prints belong to a grizzly bear; droppings close to the river let us know that otters live here. We can find out what they have been eating by identifying fish scales and bones. This tree has been damaged by grey squirrels gnawing at the bark. These burrows tell us how many sand martins are living here.

Traps

Traps are often used to remove animals when they are a nuisance, like using a mouse trap to catch mice. The gin trap is illegal in the UK.

Scientists can also use traps for sampling animal populations.

These are 'live' traps. The animal is not killed. Mice, voles and shrews can be released once the sample has been made.

Polar bears can be released far away from where people live.

Pitfall traps

Ancient people lured their prey into large holes in the ground. Gardeners sometimes prevent the damage caused by slugs and snails by setting a pitfall trap and drowning them with beer!

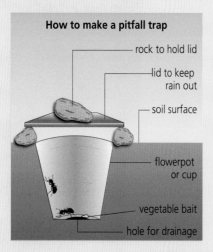

How to make a pitfall trap

- rock to hold lid
- lid to keep rain out
- soil surface
- flowerpot or cup
- vegetable bait
- hole for drainage

You can use the same approach to trap the creatures that live on the ground.

Sweep nets

Simply brush the net back and forward over a grassy area several times. Empty the contents of the net on to a white tray or sheet and examine your catch.

Pooters

You cannot suck the creatures into your mouth due to the mesh that covers the tubes. The creatures you catch in nets and traps are often small and move very quickly. The pooter allows you to trap the creatures for close examination, counting etc. before they are released.

Sampling water animals

Nets are really useful for collecting the creatures that live in streams and rivers.

Sampling land plants

You can start by simply collecting one specimen of all the different types of leaves or flowers you can find in a small area of the school grounds.

Here is a collection that was taken by one class.

Scientists are often interested in the numbers of plants that grow in particular areas. While they survey a population of plants they will also note all of the physical conditions that are found there, such as light, temperature, pH etc.

Plant mapping

By mapping where plants live you can investigate the conditions that help them survive. Is the pattern **random** or are physical factors such as light, moisture, pH etc. responsible?

Quadrats are commonly used to map plants. These may be 0.5 m square but anything will do – hula hoops, quoits, a bent wire coat hanger etc.

- Can you find any patterns between different plants growing in different places?

- Can you suggest what might affect where particular plants grow?

Samples and estimates

Businesses and political parties often sample opinions about products and policies.

When scientists want to find the number of living things, the **populations**, in a particular area they make a series of **samples**. Samples are taken in lots of different ways, such as nets and traps.

Samples are taken so that **estimates** can be carried out.

You can see that this sycamore leaf has several different types of insects living on it. It also has spots which appear in the autumn. These are caused by a fungus. It would be impossible to count the exact numbers of leaves, bugs and spots on the entire tree. Scientists **estimate** the population as accurately as they can. They often estimate the relative mass of each of the populations of living things that are found in a particular place. This is called the **biomass**.

Are there problems with the answers we find? Not really!

In all of these approaches the number of living things that you catch depends on how many of them are living there, how active they are, how far they move, as well as your skill in setting the traps and using the nets. The purpose of each approach is to make the **estimate** as accurate as possible (and to keep **errors** as low as possible).

The numbers will change from season to season and from year to year. Births and deaths will lead to changes. Some animals will leave the territory (**emigration**) and others will arrive (**immigration**).

Numeracy   + − ÷ ×

Plan how you would estimate the numbers of:

- Leaves on the tree?
- Different spots on one leaf?
- Different spots on the tree?
- Different insects living on the tree?
- Different creatures living on the tree?
- One kind of insect living on the tree?

QUESTIONS

1 Describe the most suitable ways to sample populations of each of the following:

   a) daisies on a lawn

   b) mayflies in a stream

   c) 'daddy long legs' in a meadow

   d) mice in a wood

   e) starlings in a flock.

2 Describe what happens to populations of living things when:

   a) the number of births is greater than the number of deaths

   b) the number of deaths is greater than the number of births

   c) emigration exceeds immigration.

3 What is your opinion of trapping polar bears near human communities as shown on page 8?

Biodiversity

What is biodiversity?

Biodiversity simply means the variety of living things that is found in a particular place. Scientists have identified about 1.8 million species of all living things so far but they do not know what the total number is. Their estimates vary from 5 to 100 million species.

Where is the greatest biodiversity?

The greatest variety of living things is found in the tropical rainforests.

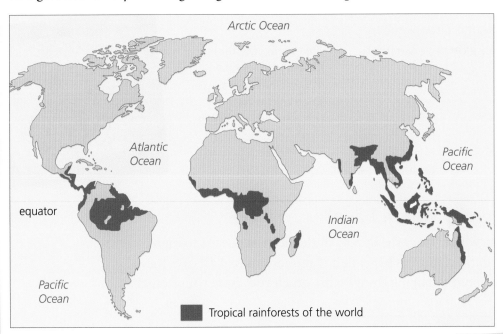

Tropical rainforests of the world

Why is biodiversity important?

All life on Earth depends on biodiversity.

The United Nations estimates that:

'At least 40% of the world's economy and 80% of the needs of the poor are derived from biological resources. In addition, the richer the diversity of life, the greater the opportunity for medical discoveries, economic development and adaptive responses to new challenges such as climate change.'

(The United Nations Convention on Biological Diversity)

Around 80% of the world's population uses medicines that are taken from plants.

Foxgloves are used to produce medicine that helps people with particular forms of heart disease.

Extinction and loss of biodiversity

Extinction, the loss of living things, is a natural process. Vast numbers of species are now extinct – maybe as many as 99% of all the living things that ever survived on Earth.

The remains of living things are often trapped in mud, soil or sand. Over thousands and millions of years these remains turn to stone and provide a record of what they once looked like. Fossil records of life on Earth show that huge numbers of different living things have appeared during the time since life began.

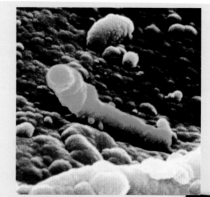

The fossilised bacteria might be as old as 3.5 billion years.

This stone contains fossils from about 400 million years ago. They might be amongst the earliest land plants.

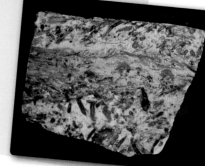

What about biodiversity where I live?

Living things are found everywhere; from the depths of the deepest oceans to high into the atmosphere; in the darkest tunnels beneath our mountains and all over the surface of the planet. Think about the living things with which you share your home.

People are a significant part of biodiversity and have the greatest impact upon it. Family pets are a familiar part of domestic biodiversity. Prey and pests share our homes. Spiders, flies and other insects are often overlooked.

Local biodiversity

With how many living things do we share the garden, school grounds and public parks?

Have you ever tried to count the numbers of different birds, trees, flowers or insects that live in your local area?

Trends and patterns

Different living things are found in different places, such as fish in water; penguins in the southern hemisphere and polar bears in the arctic north; camels and cacti in deserts etc.

When we look around we can often see that living things are restricted to particular places.

Where is the moss growing on the roof? Does it grow everywhere or is there a pattern? Look at the TV aerial. Can you see that birds use it as a perch? Their droppings land on the roof and help the moss to grow by providing water and fertiliser. You could draw a map to show where the mosses are found on this roof.

You often find this plant beside paths or growing on trampled areas at the edges of lawns. It grows flat over the surface of the grass and is not cut by lawn mowers.

We often see 'weeds' growing on the side of the road or pavement. But they're not growing everywhere, just at the side.

Scientific questions

- What might affect where these plants live?

- Is it because people do not trample the plants?

- Or because moisture is trapped there by dead leaves, twigs and litter?

- How do they survive?

- Is there enough light there?

- Do the populations change?

- If we leave them can we measure changes over a period of weeks, months and years? Would the area become overgrown with more weeds, shrubs and even trees?

When we ask these questions we are starting to study **ecology**.

QUESTIONS

1   Record the shapes of 10 different plants that are found where you live (sketch or take a photograph). Add these pictures to a class display.

2

Big numbers

Fossil remains of bacteria from 3.5 billion years ago have been found.

A billion is a big number!

a) How many thousands are there in 1 million?

b) How many millions are there in 1 billion?

c) Write 1 billion in numbers (remember, 1 million is written as 1000000).

d) Write 3.5 billion in numbers.

Identifying living things

Sorting things into groups

Gordon Buchanan is a Scottish wildlife cameraman. He has been on expeditions all around the world when new species have been found and identified. He also looks at the biodiversity that exists in Scotland.

How many living things are there?

We can quite easily count the numbers of different brands and models of cars. However, it is impossible to count the numbers of different living things that exist on Earth. This is because many of the living things are tiny and a lot of the world remains unexplored.

Roughly 1.8 million species have been properly recorded and identified. Scientists estimate that between 5 and 100 million species actually exist. They have identified 290,000 different kinds of plants.

$\Rightarrow$

Identification databases

Scientists keep the information on all known things in identification databases. Databases are computer records which maintain a lot of information in different categories.

Computers are used to store all sorts of information about groups and populations. For example, your school will have a large database that includes information about all pupils – where they live, date of birth, performance in tests etc.

Identification databases exist in a number of specialist areas, such as mammals, insects, fungi and flowering plants. Each of these is an enormous online directory that allows scientists to identify living things from entire specimens or their parts – bones, wings, spores, flowers and DNA.

Sort out that mess!

Scientists have organised all living things into different groups. The main ones are Animals, Plants, Fungi, **Protists** and **Bacteria**.

Hawthorns belong to a group of plants that are found all around the northern hemisphere.

The hawthorn is a flowering plant and it produces seeds. This helps us to separate it from a lot of different plants like mosses and ferns. This narrows the search a little bit from about 300,000 plants to 260,000 flowering plants!

Botanists group the hawthorn in the rose family. They do this because they have many similarities with the flowers and fruits of other members of the rose family. This narrows the search down to around 2500 species. The fruit is similar to the stones that you find in plums and peaches and this helps to narrow the search down further. There are only about 200 members of this group.

Final identification is made when you look at the fruit and find that it contains just one seed.

The Millennium Seed Bank

This conservation project collects and stores seeds from around the world. Seeds are cleaned, dried and identified. They are stored at a sub-zero temperature. From time to time, some seeds from each collection are germinated to make sure that they are still alive and when the collection becomes too small the seeds are grown through the plant's entire life cycle to produce new seeds.

The project aims to maintain a seed store of all known plants.

This helps conserve the plant if it is at risk of becoming extinct. It also helps if a particular plant has useful properties that scientists want to exploit, such as in the production of new foods and medicines.

QUESTIONS

1 Collect leaves from six different trees. Describe the differences that exist between them.

2 Plan the headings that you could use in a database to identify individual items in one of the following:

   a) family cars

   b) pupils in your school

   c) countries of the world

   d) garden birds

   e) supermarket fruits and vegetables.

3 Find out more about:

   a) how to store seeds

   b) local biodiversity action plans

   c) the Millennium Seed Bank.

Distribution and habitats

The Scottish landscape

The Scottish landscape helps to attract tourists. Loch Lomond is less than 20 miles from Glasgow city centre. People use the loch for sailing and fishing. The surrounding countryside is used for farming, forestry and walking. Many visitors simply admire the scenery. Loch Lomond is the largest freshwater loch in the British Isles and provides drinking water for most of central Scotland. Ben Lomond is popular with people who want to climb a 'Munro', a mountain that is higher than 3000 ft (914.4 m).

The landscape did not always look this way.

400 million years ago the Scottish mountains were part of a huge mountain chain. They were higher than the Alps and stretched for hundreds of miles. Over millions of years Scotland was shaped by dramatic events including continents crashing together, active volcanoes pouring molten rock across the land, glaciers carving the valleys, as well as the effect of changing climate. Did you know that Scotland once lay on the equator? Rainfall, rivers, floods and the sea have each changed the appearance of our landscape.

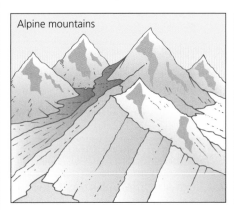
Alpine mountains

Glacial valley

Looking at habitats – a case study of Ben Lawers

There are lots of different landscapes in Scotland. They all have particular features due to the nature of the rock, soil and water which is found there. Ben Lawers lies on the north side of Loch Tay in Perthshire. It is one of Scotland's highest mountains and is owned by the National Trust for Scotland. It is a **National Nature Reserve** and this means that the area is specially protected for nature conservation.

Communities of plants and animals form food chains and food webs in every habitat.

All food chains depend on surviving in the local conditions. Plants need light, the correct temperature, the right amount of water and a number of other **physical factors** to grow properly.

Ben Lawers supports special arctic-alpine vegetation. As the name suggests these are plants which are found in the far north or high in the European mountains. The rare plants that grow here are adapted to living on the mountains. It is an extreme environment with wide ranging conditions.

Physical factors – Light

Light quality

Few trees are found on the mountain. Elsewhere trees provide shade from the sun and shelter from the wind.

These flowers grow in spring when the light intensity is lower than it is in the summer. Bluebells usually finish flowering before the leaves have fully appeared on the surrounding trees.

Day-length

Scotland lies quite far north and this means that we have very long days in mid-summer and very short ones in the middle of the winter.

Bird migration is controlled by day-length. These geese spend the winter in Britain and breed in Iceland and Greenland. They 'know' when to return to their breeding grounds as the day-length increases in spring.

Physical factors – Temperature

Have you ever noticed that snow remains on the highest hills after it has melted everywhere else? This is because the higher you go the colder it becomes. The temperature at the top of Ben Lawers (1214 m) can be as much as 8° C below the temperature at sea level.

The mountain plants that are found on Ben Lawers experience a very short growing season because spring arrives late and autumn arrives early. Plants tend to be small and grow over the surface of the ground or are found in cracks between the rocks where they are sheltered by other rocks and boulders. This helps them to collect as much heat as possible. These plants often have deep, thick roots that anchor them to the ground, helping to resist the strongest wind.

Physical factors – Water

Arctic alpine plants grow on thin soils and often grow in clumps to reduce water loss.

Physical factors – Minerals

Farmers add fertiliser to their crops to improve crop growth by adding chemical **nutrients** such as nitrogen, potassium and phosphorus. Lots of alpine plants grow on Ben Lawers because of the minerals that are released from its rock – calcium, magnesium and sodium in particular.

Biotic factors – Living things

Living things influence the landscape as well.

Biotic factors – Grazing

The main reason that trees do not grow on much of Ben Lawers is due to sheep and deer eating any tree seedlings that might appear. Trees tend to be restricted to cliff ledges and the other places that grazing animals cannot reach.

Biotic factors – The influence of mankind

People have lived in Scotland for more than 9000 years. Our influence on parts of the landscape has been enormous. We have removed the great Caledonian forest, drained large areas to create farmland and removed large areas of natural habitats.

QUESTIONS

There are many Scottish landscapes e.g. coast, islands, estuaries, moorland, farmland, lochs, rivers, woodland, forest, towns and cities. Research **one** of these landscapes, or select your own, and prepare a case study. Remember to include descriptions of a range of physical factors. Headings might include light, temperature, minerals, pH, currents, minerals and any other factors that you think are important. You might also include comments on how man has influenced your chosen landscape and how other animals and plants have affected it as well.

A little bit more

Look out for lichens

Lichens live on rock, walls, gravestones, paving stones, tree bark and even survive amongst heather on moors. Many people walk past and ignore them, and some even work hard to power wash them from their pathways.

Lichens include two kinds of living things, a fungus and an alga, living together so that both gain from the partnership. The green alga makes the food and the fungus holds water to stop them from drying out. Both living things benefit and are able to live together on exposed habitats where neither could survive on their own.

Fossils show us that lichens lived in Scotland as long as 400 million years ago. They are a surprising example of Scotland's biodiversity, with approximately 1500 species appearing in many forms and shapes, growing in the cool, moist atmosphere. Common names include Old Man's Beard, Dog Lichen and Goblin Lights.

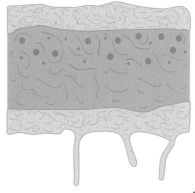

Microscopic section of a 'typical' lichen

$\Rightarrow$

A little bit more

There are three types of lichen: crusty, leafy and shrubby. Lichens can be found in a variety of colours, shapes and forms. They can be green, orange, yellow, grey, red, pink, white and black.

Lichen has been used to produce 'Crottle', the name given to dyes for Harris Tweed and kilts. Litmus, a pH indicator, is a water-soluble mixture of different dyes extracted from lichens.

Lichens are sensitive to atmospheric pollution. They can be used to indicate the level of sulphur dioxide pollution in the air.

Active Learning ▶

Activity

As long ago as 1864, Isaac Carroll studied and recorded the presence of lichen on Ben Lawers. Your challenge is to act like Carroll and the rest of the **lichenologists**. Don't walk away; 'Look out for Lichens'. Try sampling the lichens in your area. Note their colour, shape, size, abundance and what they are growing on. Note also light intensity, moisture levels and other plants growing nearby.

What is soil?

Soil, earth, dirt, or whatever you call it, is the material that covers the surface of the planet. Here's what the soil looks like when you dig down into it.

Soil horizons

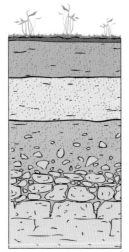

Plants are found on the surface of the soil but their roots grow deep into it.

Crops grow in the soil.

Lots of living things are found in the soil – e.g. moles, earthworms, and insects. One teaspoon of soil can contain as many as a billion bacteria!

The soil makes gases e.g. carbon dioxide by respiration. It is also an important carbon store.

Some of the living things in the soil are able to turn nitrogen from the atmosphere into useful chemicals.

Chemicals dissolve in water and drain through the soil.

Waste material decomposes in the soil.

Most of our homes are built directly onto the soil surface. Engineers compact large masses of soil when they are building roads.

What is soil?

Soil is a complicated mixture of living and non-living materials, the remains of living things, air and mineral nutrients.

When you carefully examine a handful of soil you often see roots and other pieces of plant material. You sometimes find earthworms, insects and other **invertebrates**. Small stones and pebbles make up part of the soil. When you rub soil between your fingers you can feel rough sand grains. You can squeeze it into a ball, forcing the air out. Soil usually feels moist because it holds on to a certain amount of water.

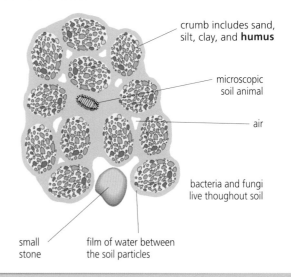

crumb includes sand, silt, clay, and **humus**

microscopic soil animal

air

bacteria and fungi live thoughout soil

small stone

film of water between the soil particles

How is soil made?

We know something about what is in the soil but how is it made?

Soil starts off as rock which is **weathered** into smaller and smaller particles. The speed at which weathering takes place depends on:

- the parent material (rock)
- time
- climate
- biological factors.

Physical (or mechanical) weathering

The rocks and stones on this scree slope have been physically broken from the **parent rock**.

Temperature changes

When rocks warm up and cool down they expand and contract. This can cause them to fracture and break.

Water

Water is unusual because it expands when it freezes. When water enters tiny fractures and cracks in the rock it freezes and then expands. This applies a physical force which helps to break the rock.

Water can also help the process of physical weathering when stones are knocked against each other by currents in rivers and oceans.

Chemical weathering

Rocks change chemically when they are exposed to the environment. Water and temperature are the main factors involved in chemical weathering.

Acid rain

All rain is slightly acidic. This is because carbon dioxide (CO_2), a naturally occurring atmospheric gas, dissolves in water (H_2O) and forms carbonic acid (H_2CO_3). Carbonic acid reacts chemically with rock, turning it into substances that can dissolve in water.

Chemical Equation

Carbon dioxide + Water → Carbonic acid

$$CO_2 \quad + \quad H_2O \quad \rightarrow \quad H_2CO_3$$

Oxidation

Oxidation takes place when oxygen reacts with the elements that are present in rocks to produce oxides. Metal oxides are often coloured such as iron oxides are rust coloured. Copper oxides are blue-green in colour. Many oxides are ores from which metals are extracted. Metal oxides which have been formed from oxidised rock are often used as glaze on pottery.

Biological factors

Soil contains huge numbers of living things – you are probably familiar with the large ones such as moles, earthworms, slugs and burrowing insect grubs. Tiny soil animals can only be seen with a microscope.

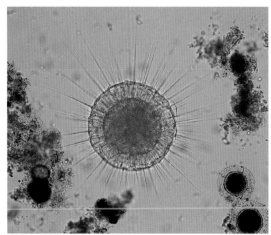

How is soil made?

Plants are anchored to the soil by their roots which help to bind the soil together and prevent further erosion. Microscopic roots grow into the tiniest soil spaces in the search for water and nutrients. Huge numbers of fungi, bacteria and **protists** affect soil fertility and development.

Living things in the soil carry out **respiration**, the biological process that leads to carbon dioxide (CO_2) production. This makes carbonic acid which will lower the **pH** and accelerate the weathering process.

Collecting soil

This often involves hard work! All you need to do is dig a hole in the ground. A metre is usually deep enough so that you can see the different horizontal layers of soil.

Road works and construction often leave exposed soil profiles available for inspection.

Sampling soil

It is easier just to look at a sample of soil taken from the surface. We can simply collect it with a garden trowel.

Take a sample from the top 10 cm with a trowel, immediately place it in a self sealing plastic bag to keep it fresh.

Deeper samples can be taken with a soil auger. This is like a corkscrew which allows you to drill into the soil, as deep as a metre, and pull a cylinder out of the soil.

QUESTIONS

1 Make lists of each of the following:

   a) living things that are found in soil

   b) weathering agents that breakdown rock

   c) chemicals that are found in soil

   d) the layers that exist in soil

   e) ways to collect soil.

Investigating soil

Lots of opportunities exist for investigating soil. You can choose to look at any of the biological, chemical, or physical aspects of the soil.

Here's a list of topics that you can choose from but you might want to carry out an investigation into something else that you think is worth investigating.

My investigation on soil pH

Here are some of the questions that I might ask:

The chemicals present in soil

Fertility

The volume of air

Soil colour

Horizons

Moisture

My investigation

Drainage

Salinity

Soil Biology

Particle size distribution

Structure

Temperature

Texture

What is pH and what about soil pH?

How can I measure pH? (Are these approaches suitable for using outdoors or do I need to bring samples to the laboratory?)

What might affect the soil pH? (Drainage. exposure to sun, slope, parent rock, colour of soil, the number of living things contained within it etc.)

Do all soils have the same pH? (Does it change in different habits? Does a flower bed have the same pH as a lawn?)

Is plant life affected by pH?

Does it change during the day or in different seasons?

You will think of your own questions for your own investigation.

GLOSSARY

Bacteria a type of micro-organism

Biodiversity the number and variety of living things found within a particular area

Biomass the mass of living material in a habitat

Biotic factors to do with life or living things

Botanist a scientist who specialises in plant science – botany

Community all the populations in a given habitat

Ecology the scientific study of the distribution and abundance of living things and way they relate to the environment

Emigration to leave one region to settle in another

Erode carried away by gravity or water

Error the difference between a measurement and the correct value

Estimate the judgment or calculation of a value in science and mathematics

Extinction a species of living things that has died out

Habitat the natural environment of a living thing

Humus soil organic material formed by the breakdown of living things

Immigration to enter and settle in a region to which the species is not native

Invertebrates animals without backbones

National Nature Reserve a government conservation designation for a location of special scientific interest

Nutrients mineral and other inorganic compounds which assist plant growth e.g. calcium and magnesium

Parent rock rock from which a soil has been formed

pH scale that measures the acidity, neutrality or alkalinity of a solution ranging from 0 to 14

Physical factor to do with the non-living part of the environment e.g. water, pH etc.

Population all the individuals of one species in a given area

Protist microscopic, usually single celled, waterborne living things

Random without any order

Quadrat a square or rectangular area for the study of plants and animals – can vary from a few centimetres to several kilometres

Respiration chemical process carried out by living things to release energy from food; releases waste carbon dioxide

Samples part of a population

Weathering chemical or mechanical processes that cause rock to break down

PLANET EARTH
Biodiversity and Interdependence

What came first, the chicken or the eggplant?

Level 2 — What came before?

 SCN 2-02a

I can use my knowledge of the interactions and energy flow between plants and animals in ecosystems, food chains and webs. I have contributed to the design or conservation of a wildlife area.

 SCN 2-02b

Through carrying out practical activities and investigations, I can show how plants have benefited society.

 SCN 2-17a

Having explored the substances that make up Earth's surface, I can compare some of their characteristics and uses.

Level 3 — What is this chapter about?

 SCN 3-02a

I have collaborated on investigations into the process of photosynthesis and I can demonstrate my understanding of why plants are vital to sustaining life on Earth.

 SCN 3-17b

I can participate in practical activities to extract useful substances from natural resources.

What came first, the chicken or the eggplant?

Thinking about this question might help you to realise the importance of all green plants in sustaining life on Earth. The eggplant, or aubergine, like all other green plants, carries out a very important chemical reaction called photosynthesis (pronounced photo-sin-the-sis).

Photosynthesis is carried out in the cells of the green parts of plants, such as the leaves, and produces oxygen gas which is released into the air. This oxygen is essential for life on Earth. So what is the answer to the question? It has to be the eggplant! Without plants to photosynthesise, animals like the chicken would not be able to survive.

Green plants: vital to keeping the Earth's atmosphere in balance

The Earth's atmosphere is made up of a mixture of gases.

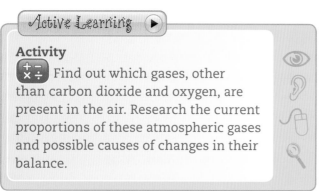

Active Learning ▶

Activity

Find out which gases, other than carbon dioxide and oxygen, are present in the air. Research the current proportions of these atmospheric gases and possible causes of changes in their balance.

Each gas makes up a particular proportion of the air so that a fine balance between each of them is achieved naturally. The reactions of respiration and photosynthesis, which are carried out by living things, maintain this balance so that the Earth's atmosphere doesn't normally change.

The proportions of the gases in the atmosphere are important for maintaining the **habitats** of many species.

Scientists, politicians and the public are concerned about small increases in levels of atmospheric carbon dioxide that have been recorded during the past 200 years. Human activities, for example in industry, farming and construction, have resulted in these changes.

Carbon dioxide is being released, principally from burning fossil fuels. At the same time large areas of rainforest are being cleared. Removing green plants from the process disturbs the part of the cycle that uses up carbon dioxide and releases oxygen back into the air.

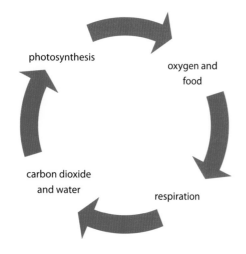

photosynthesis

oxygen and food

respiration

carbon dioxide and water

Green plants: vital to keeping the Earth's atmosphere in balance

One problem associated with the removal of green plants on such a large scale is that carbon dioxide gas begins to build up in the Earth's atmosphere. Carbon dioxide, **CO$_2$**, traps heat energy close to the planet's surface. This is known as the **Greenhouse Effect** because the gas acts like glass in a greenhouse, trapping heat inside. The effect has led to the temperature of the Earth rising slightly over time. This is known as **global warming** and it is already causing damage to several habitats on the planet.

Carbon offsetting

The population of the earth is rapidly increasing and so is the amount of CO$_2$ released into the atmosphere. Both of these factors affect the carbon cycle and it is becoming imbalanced as a result.

Three approaches are being taken:

- Reducing carbon emissions by developing alternative sources of electricity (wind, wave power etc.) and reducing waste.

- **Offsetting** carbon emissions by planting trees that will convert CO$_2$ into oxygen.

- Developing energy saving strategies such as recycling.

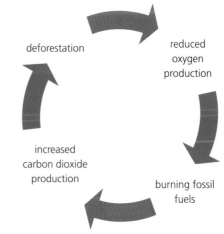

deforestation → reduced oxygen production → burning fossil fuels → increased carbon dioxide production → deforestation

Hamilton Grammar pupils raised £5000 as part of their eco-schools project to establish a mango plantation in Ghana.

QUESTIONS

1 Complete each of the following sentences:

   a) Plants use ____ and ____ to make ____ and ____ . This process is called ____ .

   b) Respiration in living things uses ____ and ____ to obtain energy.It releases ____ and ____ into the atmosphere.

   c) The processes ____ and ____ provide raw materials for each other.

2 Do you think that offsetting carbon and planting trees is a good idea?

   a) Give an advantage of this tree planting.

   b) Give one disadvantage of this.

   c) Describe any other advantages or disadvantages.

Investigating photosynthesis

Green plant cells combine carbon dioxide from the air and water in the soil into food and oxygen using light energy from the sun.

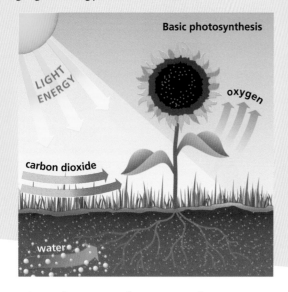

Basic photosynthesis

LIGHT ENERGY

oxygen

carbon dioxide

water

The food that is made by photosynthesis provides energy for the plant to grow and to carry out all its living processes e.g. produce flowers, fruits and seeds. Oxygen is released into the atmosphere because too much of it would poison the plant!

Plants have a green chemical, or **pigment**, called chlorophyll (pronounced klow-row-fill), which traps the energy from sunlight. Chlorophyll and light energy are said to be the **essential requirements** of the photosynthesis reaction.

The food is a carbohydrate; a sugar called glucose. This is made by combining molecules of carbon dioxide and water, the raw materials of photosynthesis. If there is too much glucose at any time it can be stored in the plant, as starch.

Testing leaves for starch

Practice the following technique to test leaves for starch:

WEAR SAFETY GOGGLES

1 – The leaf is cut off

2 – and softened in boiling water for one minute

3 – the Bunsen burner is turned off and the leaf is then warmed in alcohol to remove the green chlorophyll

Iodine

4 – the leaf is removed from the alcohol and iodine is used to test for starch

brown areas – no starch

Iodine

blue/black areas – starch is present

5 – the result shows that there is no starch present where the leaf had been covered.

Thinking about variables – what might affect plants making starch?

Light is needed for photosynthesis. Plants receive light from the sun. Photosynthesis will not take place if a plant is in darkness.

Carbon dioxide is needed for photosynthesis. Plants receive carbon dioxide from the air.

??? is needed for photosynthesis.

??? is needed for photosynthesis.

??? is needed for photosynthesis.

??? is needed for photosynthesis.

??? is needed for photosynthesis.

What happens to photosynthesis if plants are deprived of water? This can only be investigated using radioactive water (not allowed in schools) as plants die if they have no water.

QUESTIONS

1 Photosynthesis is a chemical process that takes place inside green plants.

   a) What carbohydrate is made during photosynthesis?

   b) Which carbohydrate is stored in plants?

   c) Which materials **are used** during the process?

   d) Which gas **is made**?

2 Write the word equation that summarises photosynthesis. (Here is one that describes respiration: Food + oxygen → Carbon dioxide + water + energy)

3 Identify variables that might affect photosynthesis.

Photosynthesis factories

The structure of a green leaf makes it a very efficient photosynthesis 'factory'. There are pores on the surface, particularly the lower surface called **stomata**. These allow the carbon dioxide gas to be absorbed from the air. The gas enters spaces in the layers of cells in the leaf and **diffuses** into the palisade cells that contain lots of green **chloroplasts**. The palisade cells are close to the upper surface of the leaf where light can enter and be absorbed by the chlorophyll that is inside the chloroplasts.

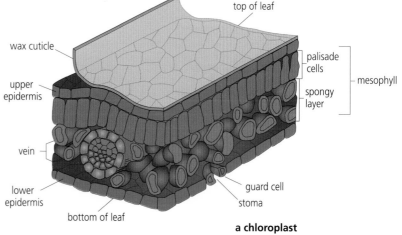

top of leaf
wax cuticle
upper epidermis
vein
lower epidermis
bottom of leaf
palisade cells
mesophyll
spongy layer
guard cell
stoma

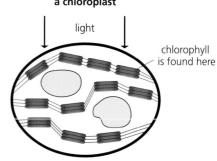

a chloroplast

light

chlorophyll is found here

The great search for water

It is vital that plants are able to find a source of water as it is a raw material for photosynthesis. Roots grow downwards from seeds into the ground to find water. This happens at the earliest stage of germination. As they grow, **root hairs** emerge and absorb water by **osmosis**.

The water is transported from the roots to the leaves so that it can be used for photosynthesis in mesophyll cells.

water leaves through stoma and evaporates

water replaced from inner cells

water pulled up through the xylem

roots take in more water

The movement of water upwards through the plant roots and stems to the leaves is called **transpiration**. There are special vessels that carry the water through the plant called **xylem** (pronounced zigh-lem). Water enters the leaves through the **leaf veins** and water can then be absorbed by the photosynthesising cells.

QUESTIONS

1 Write a sentence to explain steps 2 and 3 in the procedure for testing leaves for starch, shown on page 28.

2 Design and carry out an experiment to investigate the effect of temperature on photosynthesis.

And there's more – energy flow

Photosynthesis doesn't just produce food for the plant. It also provides food for us! Humans and other animals cannot photosynthesise so they can't make their own food. Instead, we rely on plants converting light energy into chemical energy during photosynthesis. Once the chemical energy, or carbohydrate, is stored in the plant, it may be eaten by animals. In this way, **herbivores** get the energy they need. These animals can then be eaten by other animals and some of the energy (that isn't used or wasted) is 'passed on'.

This flow of energy through living things is called a food chain. Without green plants photosynthesising, animals would have no food.

Food chains and food webs

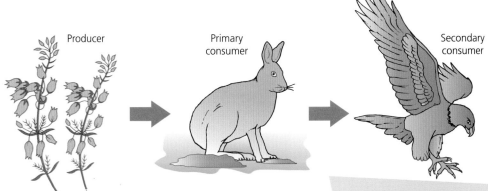

Producer

Primary consumer

Secondary consumer

The producer is a green plant. It makes its own food by photosynthesis. Consumers eat and digest food from plants or other animals.

Food chains become inter-connected because animals usually have more than one choice of food.

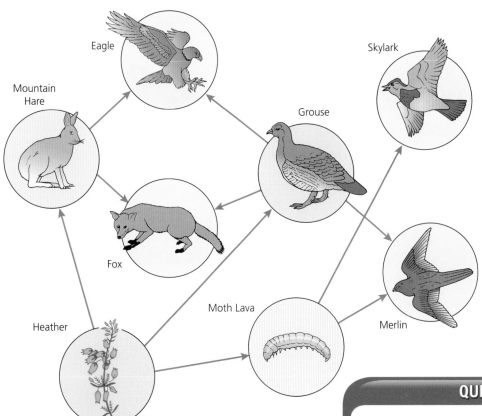

Eagle

Mountain Hare

Skylark

Grouse

Fox

Moth Lava

Merlin

Heather

Within a food web, there is **interdependence**. This means that all living things are involved in feeding relationships, either as **predators** or as **prey** and these relationships are very important to the survival of each of the species that are living together in one place.

QUESTIONS

1 What name is given to animals that eat:

   a) plants

   b) other animals

   c) both.

2 What might animals use energy for?

3 How might energy be 'lost' in a food chain?

We use plants for food

We use plants for housing

We use plants for entertainment

We use plants for clothing

We use plants as consumer goods

We use plants for medicine

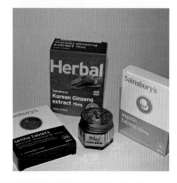

We use plants for travel

We use plants for sport

We use plants for energy

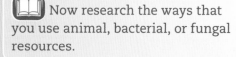

Active Learning ▶

Activity

Now research the ways that you use animal, bacterial, or fungal resources.

GLOSSARY

Carbon offsetting ways of balancing increasing CO_2 levels in the atmosphere

Chloroplast structure found in algal and green plant cells containing chlorophyll

Diffuse process that leads to chemical substances spreading through liquid or gas

Global warming an increase in the planet's average temperature over time

Greenhouse Effect the process of trapping heat from the Sun in the atmosphere

Habitat the natural environment of a living thing

Herbivore an animal that eats plant material

Interdependence living things that depend on each other

Osmosis process in living things that allows water to diffuse in and out of cells

Photosynthesis chemical process that takes place in the chloroplasts of plant cells

Pigment a coloured chemical

Predator a living thing that survives by consuming other living things

Prey a living thing that is eaten by others

Root hair cell that is capable of growing into tiny soil spaces and absorbing water

Stomata pores found on the surface of leaves – singular 'stoma'

Transpiration process brought about by evaporation of water from a leaf that draws water through the entire plant

Xylem tissue that carries water and dissolved substances upward through plants

PLANET EARTH
Biodiversity and Interdependence

Chemicals and living things

Level 2   What came before?

 SCN 2-03a

I have collaborated in the design of an investigation into the effects of fertilisers on the growth of plants. I can express an informed view of the risks and benefits of their use.

Level 3   What is this chapter about?

 SCN 3-03a

Through investigation, and based on experimental evidence, I can explain the use of different types of chemicals in agriculture and their alternatives and can evaluate their potential impact on the world's food production.

Chemicals and living things

All living organisms are made of cells, but what are cells made of? Cells, like all materials on the planet, are made from chemical elements and their compounds.

Elements and compounds

There are nearly a hundred different naturally occurring chemical **elements**, pure substances which combine to make every **compound**.

Only four of those elements make almost all the compounds that are found in living things. Another 22 elements are found in very small quantities.

CHON

The main elements found in living organisms are carbon (C), hydrogen (H), oxygen (O) and nitrogen (N) (CHON = Carbon, Hydrogen, Oxygen and Nitrogen). These elements combine in different ways to make three main groups of compounds that are found in living organisms:

Carbohydrates	Proteins	Lipids

Elements and compounds

Almost all the chemical compounds that are found in a plant are made from water and carbon dioxide which are available to the plant from the soil and the air. Plants are called **autotrophs**.

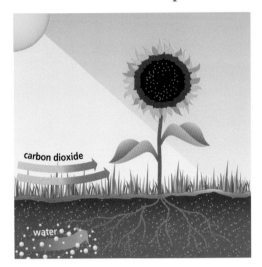

carbon dioxide

water

Water and carbon dioxide contain only three elements – carbon, hydrogen and oxygen – and plants need tiny quantities of other elements to make other compounds. For example, the chemical chlorophyll (pronounce klow-row-fill), which makes leaves appear green, contains the element magnesium. Plants get magnesium and other mineral elements from soil minerals. Minerals are absorbed, dissolved in water, through the plant roots, and are used to build the chemicals needed by plants.

The mineral nutrients present in soil are essential for the growth of plants.

Plants sometimes store high levels of minerals inside their tissues. This can sometimes be used to help prospecting for ores.

If the soil is lacking in any particular nutrient then the plants growing in it will lack essential chemicals and not be healthy.

Animals must eat other organisms in order to obtain their food. Digestion breaks down food into useful chemical building blocks. Animals are unable to make food in the same way as plants – they process the chemicals during **metabolism**. Animals are called **heterotrophs**.

QUESTIONS

1 Explain why plants growing in a soil with low levels of magnesium have yellow leaves.

2 List three plants that are used to produce **carbohydrate**-rich foods.

3 List three plants that are used to produce **protein**-rich foods.

4 List three plants that are used to produce **lipid**-rich foods.

Organic food

ORGANIC
Organic
Oranges
2.99 LB

What does it mean when food is labelled as organic? The difference between organically produced food and non-organic food is that organic farmers use fewer chemicals. Is organic food a better choice? In order to make this decision we have to find out about the chemicals used in farming. Farmers who grow crops use two main types of chemical: fertilisers and pesticides.

Fertilisers

Fertilisers contain the mineral nutrients needed by plants. Fertilisers help plants to grow and are used by farmers, horticulturalists and gardeners. All plants need elements, including nitrogen to make proteins, magnesium to make chlorophyll and a range of other elements such as potassium for protein synthesis and phosphorous for membranes and DNA. These are essential for the plant to make the compounds it needs. Without these minerals the plant would be unhealthy and could not grow in a particular area. Crops depend on the correct minerals being present for their growth.

Chemical	Use	Signs when this chemical is missing
Nitrogen	To make proteins and DNA	Leaves and shoots will be smaller than normal, brown leaves
Phosphorous	To make important plant chemicals	Yellow spots on leaves
Potassium	Needed for plant chemical reactions	Poor growth, purple leaves

QUESTIONS

1 Look at the plant in the photograph. This plant is growing in an environment that lacks an important substance.

   a) Describe the appearance of the plant.

   b) Explain which substance you think is missing from the plant's environment?

2 How do organically grown crops receive the mineral nutrients which are essential for their healthy growth?

Farming and the environment

When farmers harvest their crops they remove nutrients from that area. The crops absorb minerals from the soil but these minerals are not replaced. The soil will slowly begin to run out of minerals. This is called soil depletion. To prevent this happening farmers apply fertiliser to their fields. In the past, before the development of the agro-chemical industry, farmers tried to prevent mineral depletion by practices such as crop rotation.

Farmers regularly spread their fields with fertilisers. Natural fertilisers (green fertilisers) include manure and rotted plant matter – **compost**. Artificial fertilisers dissolve in the soil water before being absorbed by the plants roots. These return nutrients to the soil. By doing this, farmers ensure that their crops are healthy and grow well.

Farming and the environment

Large amounts of fertiliser are made in chemical factories. The process uses energy and releases carbon dioxide into the atmosphere. It also produces other pollutants.

Benefits of fertiliser

The application of fertiliser produces higher yielding plants that can be harvested year after year.

The effect of fertiliser on a river

When it rains some of the dissolved fertiliser is washed away into rivers and streams. This process is called **leaching**.

Excess fertiliser in a river can lead to a reduction in oxygen levels. When the fertiliser drains into rivers and lakes it causes increased growth of microscopic plant life – algae.

The algae become overgrown and they are unable to compete for light. They die and become food for bacteria. A food chain becomes established and the bacteria grow and multiply. Increased bacterial numbers use up oxygen when they **respire**. This reduces the oxygen concentration and fish and invertebrates die or move away.

Feed the world?

The world population is increasing. In many parts of the world farmers are unable to produce enough food to feed the local population. Animal manure is often dried and used as fuel for cooking. Fertiliser can help to increase crop production and this could reduce the numbers of people suffering starvation.

Is there an alternative to fertiliser use?

Different plants remove different minerals from the soil. During the eighteenth century European farmers introduced crop rotation to increase the productivity of the land. Crop rotation and mechanisation are part of the '**agrarian revolution**'. Rotations involve growing different crops over a planned sequence of seasons. This helps the natural recovery of the soil's nutrient resources. Farmers also found that including clover in the rotation improved soil fertility and the wheat yield the following year.

Clover and other members of the pea family turn atmospheric nitrogen and oxygen into nitrate compounds which help other plants to grow. Animals grazing on the clover will release manure on the pasture and this helps as well.

QUESTIONS

1 Use the information on the previous page to draw a flowchart or diagram explaining the effect of fertiliser on a river.

2 How do plants growing in the wild obtain essential chemicals such as nitrates?

3 Find out about crop rotation and green manure as ways of reducing fertiliser use.

4 Scientists breed plants for particular characteristics e.g. increased yield, disease resistance, flavour etc. Find out how they do this by:

   a) selective breeding **or**

   b) genetic modification.

Plant pests and pesticide use

Pests are organisms that humans consider to be a problem. Some insects eat crops and reduce the yield. Plants can also be damaged by fungal attack or face competition from weeds.

Stored crops can also provide food for pests e.g. mice, insects and fungi.

Food stores provide shelter, warmth and, of course, food for many different pests.

These diseased potato leaves are suffering from 'blight' fungus. Between 1845 and 1849 as many as a million Irish people died as a result of starvation and disease caused by potato blight.

Plant pests and pesticide use

Farmers use chemicals called pesticides to remove pest populations e.g. rat poison. They may use a wide variety of pesticides.

Insecticides are used to kill insect pests. As well as killing plant pests they often kill all other insects. Some of these insects may have been useful to farmers because they were predators of some of the plant pests or might have been pollinators.

Herbicides are used to kill weeds. Some herbicides that enter the soil are broken down by micro-organisms to harmless chemicals quite quickly but others last in the soil for a long time.

Fungicides are used to kill fungi (mould). Farmers can spray their fields regularly with these chemicals and continue to apply fungicides after the crop has been harvested. Fungicides may contain elements such as copper or mercury which can be poisonous to other organisms, including humans.

Impact on food chains

Organisms in an ecosystem are interdependent through their connections to each other. Adding pesticides can have an impact throughout the ecosystem. Our food contains minute amounts of these chemicals.

Organic farming

Organic farmers and gardeners do not apply artificial chemicals to their crops.

Pests are controlled with rotations, cultivation and other natural means.

QUESTIONS

1   Find out more about the famine in Ireland during the nineteenth century. Write up your findings in a short report.

2   Find out about biological pest control. What is it and what are the benefits of this method of pest control?

Down on the farm

The impact of people on the planet has been greater than any other species. This includes our methods of food production. Clearing land for farming significantly alters the ecosystem, removes habitats and decreases food sources for wildlife. Chemicals used by farmers pollute rivers and kill plants and animals. The increased use of machinery and chemicals on farms has reduced the manpower but increased the energy use by farms, contributing significantly to rising carbon dioxide levels.

Another problem with modern intensive farming methods is that land may be used to grow non-food crops such as tea, tobacco and coffee. These so-called 'cash crops' grow on land that could be used to grow food.

Down on the farm

Scientists are trying to find some solutions to the problems of the increasing human population and the environmental impact of food production.

- Plants with higher yields of food are being developed.

- Organic farming methods reduce the use of chemicals.

- Plants are being developed, through the technique of genetic engineering, that require less fertiliser and pesticide use.

- However, organic produce is more expensive and some people have concerns about growing genetically modified (GM) plants.

- In developing countries traditional methods of farming such as crop rotation and **intercropping** are used.

- These methods help to reduce the depletion of soil nutrients and therefore less fertiliser is required.

QUESTIONS

1 📖 Find out about the Scottish Crop Research Institute and its work. Present your research to the class.

2 Modern farming decreases biodiversity. Explain why.

Pesticides: The DDT story

DDT is an insecticide that was used throughout the world after its introduction in the 1940s. It was very successful at controlling mosquitoes and plant pests. However, after its widespread use, problems arose. Around the world people were reporting a decline in the populations of large predatory birds such as golden eagles, peregrine falcons and ospreys.

Research by ecologists discovered that the birds had relatively high levels of the pesticide DDT in their tissues. Further research discovered that the highest levels of pesticide were found in animals at the top of the food chain, the top carnivores.

The level of insecticide was being concentrated at each step in the food chain. This is because the DDT was not being broken down at each stage in the food chain. The high levels of insecticide found in the birds were reducing their ability to reproduce. Scientists found that the shell around their eggs was becoming thinner and breaking during incubation. Consequently their numbers declined.

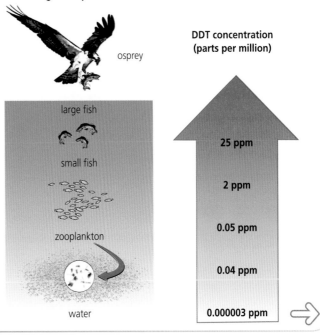

DDT concentration (parts per million)

osprey	
large fish	25 ppm
small fish	2 ppm
zooplankton	0.05 ppm
	0.04 ppm
water	0.000003 ppm

A happy ending?

Pro – banning DDT

As a result of this research DDT was banned in many countries and use of this type of pesticide was controlled. However, because these pesticides cannot be broken down by organisms and food chains they remain stored in the fat cells of many organisms. DDT has been found in the tissues of nearly every living thing on the planet, including us.

Con – banning DDT

Malaria is caused by a parasite which enters the body via the bite of the female Anopheles mosquito. We know a lot about the life cycle of the parasite, and have developed drugs to prevent and cure malaria, yet each year 300 to 500 million people are infected with malaria worldwide, leading to between 1.5 and 2.7 million deaths annually.

Indoor spraying of insecticide is the most effective means of rapidly reducing mosquito density. Indoor spraying in small quantities is effective for 3 to 6 months, depending on the insecticide used and the type of surface on which it is sprayed. (DDT is effective for longer periods, up to 12 months in some cases.) DDT is also very cheap to produce.

Nutrient cycles

In a natural environment such as a meadow or a woodland the minerals needed by plants do not run out because they are constantly recycled. The first step in this recycling is the process of decay or decomposition. Any waste produced by organisms will become food for micro-organisms, which will then break down the waste and recycle the minerals and nutrients present in the waste. Eventually when an organism dies it will be recycled by the action of micro-organisms. This recycling is essential or the soil nutrients would run out.

$\Rightarrow$

Nutrient cycles

Earthworms and other burrowing animals play a very important part in mixing soil, increasing oxygen supply and helping decomposition in the soil. The organisms that bring about decay belong to two groups: bacteria and fungi. These important micro-organisms help to recycle essential nutrients such as carbon, nitrogen and phosphorous.

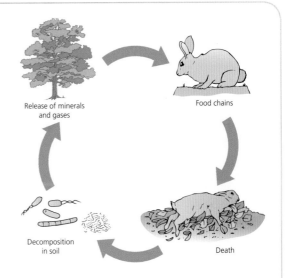

Release of minerals and gases

Food chains

Decomposition in soil

Death

QUESTIONS

1 Should DDT be banned worldwide?

2 Design an investigation into the effects of herbicides on plant growth.

3 Find out more about the nitrogen cycle.

GLOSSARY

Agrarian revolution changes in agricultural practice brought about by science and technology

Autotroph any organism that produces its own food

Carbohydrates compounds that contain only carbon, hydrogen and oxygen e.g. sugar and starch that are energy sources in the diet of animals

Compost decaying organic matter e.g. dead leaves or manure

Compound a substance composed of two or more elements

Element a substance that cannot be broken into simpler substances by chemical means

Fungicides pesticide that acts against fungi

Herbicides pesticide that acts against weeds

Heterotroph organism requiring organic food

Insecticides pesticide that acts against insects

Leach to cause a solution to drain through soil or rock

Lipid one of the main chemical groups that are found in cells

Metabolism all the chemical reactions that take place in living things

Protein one of the main chemical groups that are found in cells

Respire the process of respiration that releases chemical energy from food

PLANET EARTH
Processes of the Planet

Our life support system

Level 2 — What came before?

 SCN 2-05a

I can apply my knowledge of how water changes state to help me understand the processes involved in the water cycle in nature over time.

 SCN 2-06a

By observing and researching features of our solar system, I can use simple models to communicate my understanding of size, scale, time and relative motion within it.

Level 3 — What is this chapter about?

 SCN 3-05b

I can explain some of the processes which contribute to climate change and discuss the possible impact of atmospheric change on the survival of living things.

 SCN 3-06a

By using my knowledge of our solar system and the basic needs of living things, I can produce a reasoned argument on the likelihood of life existing elsewhere in the universe.

Our life support system

This planet that we inhabit provides us with everything we need in order to survive: food, water, oxygen and systems for removal of waste. It provides the raw materials from which everything on this planet is constructed, including us. People use the planet for raw materials but every day the number of people on the planet is increasing and the resources are limited.

The atmosphere

The layer of gases around the planet, the atmosphere, provides living organisms with the gases essential for survival. The main gases of the air are nitrogen, carbon dioxide and oxygen. The air also contains variable volumes of water vapour and traces of other gases such as argon.

Carbon dioxide

Carbon dioxide (CO_2) is present in the atmosphere in very small volumes but it is essential to life on the planet. This gas is taken in by plants and used as a building block to make food during the process of photosynthesis.

The atmosphere around our planet contains about 0.03% CO_2. Each year large quantities of this CO_2 are absorbed by plants during photosynthesis. Despite this the volume of CO_2 does not decrease. This is because CO_2 is recycled. Plants take in CO_2 for photosynthesis and use it to make food. The food will eventually be broken down, for energy, in a process called cellular respiration by the plant or by any animals that consume the plant. Cellular respiration releases CO_2 back into the atmosphere.

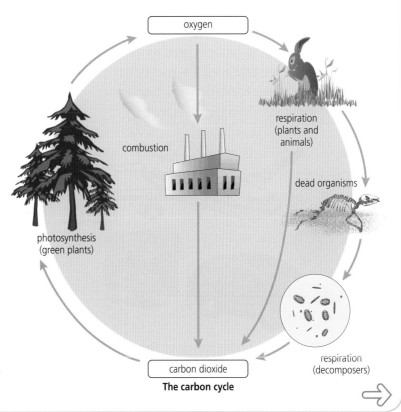

oxygen

respiration (plants and animals)

combustion

dead organisms

photosynthesis (green plants)

carbon dioxide

respiration (decomposers)

The carbon cycle

The atmosphere

Changing carbon dioxide levels

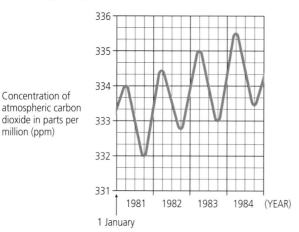

Concentration of atmospheric carbon dioxide in parts per million (ppm)

1 January

Levels of CO_2 in the atmosphere naturally change each year. Some years have higher levels than others and during each year the level changes.

Look at the diagram of the carbon cycle on the previous page.

QUESTIONS

1 List the processes that add carbon dioxide to the atmosphere.

2 Find out how much oxygen, nitrogen and carbon dioxide are present in the atmosphere.

3 What is the chemical symbol for:

   a) oxygen gas

   b) nitrogen gas

   c) carbon dioxide?

4 Study the graph showing carbon dioxide levels.

   a) Explain why carbon dioxide levels decrease in summer?

   b) What general trend does the graph show for carbon dioxide levels?

Mankind's impact on the carbon cycle

Carbon dioxide levels have been increasing in the atmosphere since the start of the industrial revolution. As mankind has invented more and more technology our need for energy has increased. Energy is needed to power our homes, to manufacture goods and for transport.

Burning fossil fuels provides much of this energy. Coal, oil, gas and peat are called fossil fuels because they were formed from the fossilised remains of dead plants and animals.

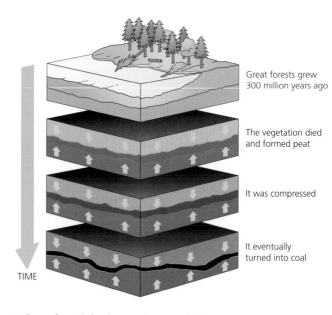

Great forests grew 300 million years ago

The vegetation died and formed peat

It was compressed

It eventually turned into coal

TIME

When fossil fuels are burned CO_2 is released into the atmosphere. Using an electrical appliance, travelling by bus or aeroplane or purchasing anything that is manufactured and transported are all activities that contribute to CO_2 levels.

Global warming and the greenhouse effect

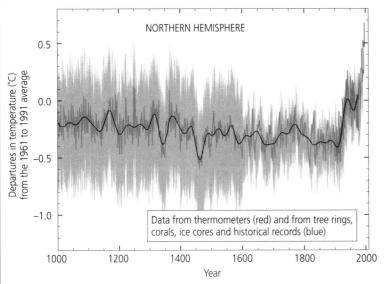

NORTHERN HEMISPHERE

Departures in temperature (°C) from the 1961 to 1991 average

Data from thermometers (red) and from tree rings, corals, ice cores and historical records (blue)

Year

In recent years most scientists have become convinced that the Earth is becoming warmer and that the annual average temperature is steadily rising. They believe that this change in climate is due to the increase in certain gases in the atmosphere and that this is due to mankind's activities. One reason for this is the Greenhouse Effect. Much of the Sun's radiation that reaches the earth is reflected back into space in the form of heat. Increased levels of CO_2 reduces the proportion of heat that is reflected back. More heat energy is retained by the Earth, causing the planet to heat up.

Sun

escaping radiation

absorbed

reflected

edge of atmosphere

absorbed by atmosphere and Earth

radiation absorbed by greenhouse gases

greenhouse gases and fossil fuels

Oil and petrol engines

deforestation

CFCs

QUESTIONS

1 Make a list of as many human activities as you can think of that will lead to CO_2 being released into the atmosphere.

2 Research the Industrial Revolution.

 a) What was it?

 b) When did it take place?

 c) What caused it?

 d) What fuelled it?

Effects of global warming

In 2003 there was a 'canicule' or heat wave in France. The French government estimated that the canicule may have caused as many as 14 000 deaths among the elderly due to dehydration. Heat waves are becoming more frequent and the global climate is changing.

Global warming is predicted to cause flooding, drought and change unproductive farmland into desert. What will be the impact on human health and wellbeing?

Reduction in food production

Flooding, drought and **desertification** will reduce the area of land available for growing food. This is already happening in parts of Africa and causes widespread famine and much human suffering. Failure of crops due to drought is common in Africa and now happens more often. Parts of Asia are also suffering severe drought and food shortages. Farmland situated beside river banks is becoming unusable as a result of the river becoming saltier. Increased global temperatures could also lead to failure of crops, as plants may dehydrate in higher than normal temperatures. People may die due to a shortage of fresh drinking water.

Ecological migrants

As farmland shrinks and shortages of water occur people will be forced to leave their homes in order to survive. These 'ecological migrants' will be dependent on others for food, water and shelter. Major charities such as Oxfam are already anticipating these problems and are becoming involved in promoting measures to reduce global warming.

Active Learning ▶

Activity

📖 Research factors leading to drought in Africa.

Write a short article on the causes of drought. Suggest ways to reduce this problem.

Carbon Footprints

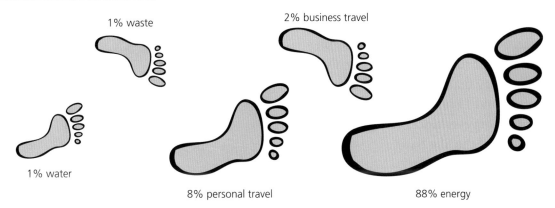

1% waste

2% business travel

1% water

8% personal travel

88% energy

We all have a **carbon footprint** because we all do activities which produce CO_2 and contribute to global warming. Reducing our carbon footprint will help to slow down climate change and could help to save lives.

Active Learning

Activity

Choose one of the examples of energy saving activities and explain how doing this would reduce your carbon footprint.

What can the government do to encourage people to have smaller carbon footprints?

The origins of the universe

Scientific study has developed our understanding of the universe. Scientists have discovered strong evidence from meteorite dating and star analysis to support the theory that the universe had a starting point around 13 billion years ago and that it has been expanding ever since. This remarkable event has been called the 'Big Bang'.

The 'Big Bang' describes when space and time were created. The universe may be defined as 'all that is or ever was or ever will be'. The universe is older and more immense than we can really imagine.

'Our wildest dreams sometimes result in our greatest endeavours.'

Humankind is a curious and imaginative species and desires to investigate the universe and reveal its mysteries. Since the earliest times humankind has looked at the sky at night and wondered if there was life somewhere out there thinking similar thoughts.

Our earth is merely one planet in the almost empty, cold, vacuum of the universe. Galaxies, stars and planets seem rare in the great expanse of vacuum. A galaxy is made of billions of stars, planets, dust and gas.

The Sun is our star. Any star that is seen in the universe may be a sun to some form of life.

On some of these planets there may be life, intelligence and technology.

'Our universe probably came into existence not only from nothing but from nowhere.' (Heather Couper, Past President of the British Astronomical Association)

Active Learning ▶

Research Activity

Research the 'Big Bang'.

Research the search for extraterrestrial life.

Discuss your findings and views with others.

Three scientists, Jennifer Loveland-Curtze, Vanya I. Miteva and Jean E. Brenchley, have discovered a purple-brown coloured bacterium 3 km beneath the ice covering Greenland. This microbe has been frozen for the last 120 000 years. The scientists believe that this **bacterium** could hold clues to the potential for life on other planets.

A really slow, gentle thawing process was undertaken over the course of a year and resulted in the bacterium **replicating** after being thawed out. This bacterium is 80% smaller than most bacteria and belongs to a group of 'ultramicro' bacteria that live in extreme environments. Conditions endured by this microbe may be similar to environments where **extraterrestrial** life may be found on planets elsewhere in the Universe. The scientists have shown that DNA and other cell structures can survive very low temperatures, e.g. $-56°C$, for great periods of time.

As well as the extreme cold, these microbes have been shown to survive high pressure, lack of space, limited oxygen and lack of nutrients. These conditions are found in the ice and are known to exist elsewhere in the universe.

This is rocket science

In 1976, America's unmanned Viking Lander was the first craft to land on the surface of Mars. The Viking missions to Mars were searching for life on another planet.

The small numbers of press and public who followed the progress of the mission were disappointed when the definitive answer to the question 'is there, or has there ever been, life on Mars' was not revealed by Viking's explorations.

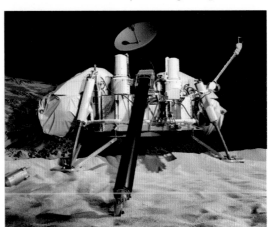

The search for life in our galaxy has involved looking for planets of other stars, searching for evidence of life on Mars and on the moons of Jupiter and Saturn and learning more about the biochemistry of life's beginnings and evolution of life on Earth.

In September 2000, Commander Terry Wilcutt led the crew of the Space Shuttle mission STS-106 to the International Space Station orbiting the Earth. The main objectives of this mission involved hooking up equipment and unpacking and stowing gear for the first resident crew.

This is rocket science

It is worth remembering that we live on a spaceship … spaceship Earth. It provides all that we require except the heat and light that comes from our Sun.

Look after it. Act locally, think globally.

We have only one Earth.

Basic needs

For life to have developed on any planet basic conditions for life have to be met.

A suitable gravitational force is essential. If it were too great then life could not exist.

Life on this planet is based on carbon and water. Water is a solvent in which chemicals dissolve. Scientists are now asking the following questions:

'Must all life forms be composed of the same carbon compounds as they are on Earth?'

'Can life that is made of other chemicals have evolved on other worlds?'

'I think it far more difficult to understand a universe in which we are the only technological civilization or one of but a few, than to imagine a cosmos brimming over with intelligent life.' (Carl Sagan)

Basic needs and life on Earth

The conditions for human survival are important to life on Earth as well. When natural disasters happen, e.g. earthquakes, people are deprived of their needs. Drinking water, food and shelter are often in short supply.

Is there life on one of Saturn's moons?

During July 2009 scientists found one of the best places in the solar system to search for alien life. The spacecraft Cassini, launched in 1997, has been orbiting Saturn since 2004. Scientists were observing images of one of Saturn's moons called Enceladus (pronounced En-Sell-Add-Us). They found jets of water vapour on the surface that may come from underground salty oceans. The gases contain salts and traces of organic materials. Liquid water, an energy source, and the right mix of chemical starting blocks are required to produce life.

The scientists might not find living things on Enceladus but they do seem to have found somewhere else in the solar system where some of the conditions required for life exist.

Think of all the things that you own.

The longest period of human existence has been spent in a time where humans owned very little and there was time, as the campfire grew dim, to look at the stars in the night sky and think. Humankind has matured on our lonely planet and is now searching for life in our solar system and beyond…

Is anyone out there?

In Scotland, cloudy skies, other interests, lack of time, a roof over our head and light pollution mean that we rarely take the opportunity to stare at the night sky in wonder.

Stare in awe, be like the 'Big Bang', and make time.

QUESTIONS

1 List all the things that are essential to human survival when we travel in space.

2 Make a table that compares the conditions described in Greenland with Saturn's moon Enceladus.

GLOSSARY

Carbon Footprint a measure of carbon dioxide production related to activities e.g. travel, consumer products etc.

Bacterium singular for bacteria

Desertification turning land into desert

Evolved changed and developed with time

Extraterrestrial living thing that has come from somewhere other than the Earth

Replicate reproduce and make an exact copy

FORCES, ELECTRICITY AND WAVES

Forces

5

Weightlessness and living things

Level 2 — What came before?

 SCN 2-08a

I have collaborated in investigations to compare magnetic, electrostatic and gravitational forces and have explored their practical applications.

Level 3 — What is this chapter about?

 SCN 3-08a

I have collaborated in investigations into the effects of gravity on objects and I can predict what might happen to their weight in different situations on Earth and in space.

Weightlessness and living things

The payload of Space Shuttle Atlantis (mission STS-129), launched during November 2009, included four experiments designed to investigate the effect of weightlessness – zero gravity – on living things. The experiments were undertaken in the Kibo laboratory of the International Space Station.

Microbes, butterflies, woody plants and roundworms were grown under weightless conditions and their growth patterns were compared with the same organisms grown on Earth.

Weightlessness is thought to have long-term effects on living things by affecting how their **genes** function. The worms suffered loss of muscle mass similar to the reduction in muscle tissue experienced by humans undertaking space flight. The aim of the experiment was to test possible treatments aimed at reducing muscle loss. This research and the results of other investigations on living things in zero gravity conditions provided valuable insights into how to deal with the effects of weightlessness on humans on long-term missions aboard the space station, on the surface of the moon (where the gravity is only one-sixth that of the Earth) or on the long journey to Mars.

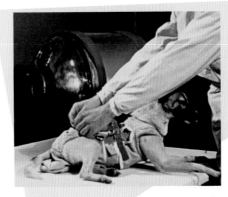

Laika was the first dog in space.

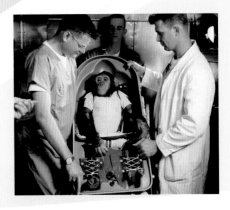

Ham was the first chimpanzee in space.

The earliest spaceflights used animals to test the ability of living things to cope with weightlessness.

Yuri Gagarin, a Russian **Cosmonaut**, became the first human in space in April 1961 when he orbited planet Earth during a space flight that lasted less than 2 hours. Since then spaceflights have greatly increased in duration and have included six **lunar** landing missions by American **Astronauts**.

From observations of astronauts during and after spaceflight it has been known for some time that weightless conditions can affect health. Some of the effects of weightlessness are short term, and others have a long-term influence on human health.

Yuri Gagarin was the first man in space.

Short-term effects – space sickness

Almost 50% of space travellers feel ill during the first hours of spaceflight. They feel sick, dizzy, get headaches, sweat and feel very tired – these are symptoms of space sickness. Its effects can last for up to three days until the body adapts to weightless conditions.

Astronauts are trained in short periods of weightlessness in an aircraft which has been nicknamed 'the vomit comet'.

Long-term effects – healthy bones

The most damaging long-term effects of zero gravity reported so far are reductions in bone structure. Loss of bone cells and minerals occurs when the physical stress placed on bones by the force of gravity is decreased or is removed completely. The reduction in the calcium content of bone is termed **osteoporosis** and its effects can be greatly reduced by exercise that places a load on the body.

The minerals absorbed from the bone may accumulate in the kidneys causing kidney stones.

Zero gravity studies focus on developing survival strategies for long-term space missions, which will include developing guidelines for the prevention of osteoporosis that will be caused by long space flights during future missions to the Moon and Mars. Frequent, energy demanding, load bearing exercise will reduce muscle and bone deterioration.

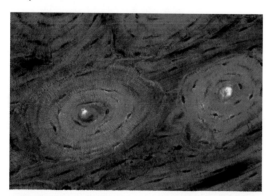

Long-term effects – healthy bones

Scientists who study the ageing process on muscle and skeleton have reported similar results to the scientists who study the effects of zero gravity on human systems. Results from experiments undertaken in space may therefore have a major impact on improving the medical care here on Earth for the elderly and for individuals confined to bed for long periods.

Body fluids

The distribution of fluid around our body is normally influenced by gravity. Zero gravity results in body fluids moving away from the lower parts of our body to the upper body and head.

The brain mistakes this increased volume of fluid in the head for an overall increase in the volume of body fluid. It then stimulates the kidneys to remove more water from the bloodstream. As a result, astronauts risk suffering from **dehydration**.

Balance

Problems with balance result when the detectors in the inner ear that allow individuals to sense gravity do not receive this information as a result of weightlessness. This produces a sense of confusion which affects co-ordination, balance and posture. After returning to Earth's gravitational pull astronauts and cosmonauts can suffer from extreme dizziness.

Astronaut Gordon Cooper felt dizzy after his space flight. He was helped out of the space capsule.

Benefits of research into the effects of weightlessness

Humans are at risk in a zero gravity environment. However, research into the human body's response to weightlessness may help the elderly to live better quality lives. The ageing process and long space flights have similar effects on health.

Elderly people experience weakening bones and muscles, difficulties with sleeping and a reduced immune response. The main difference between the symptoms of old age and long exposure to conditions of weightlessness is that the changes endured by space travellers are generally reversible. There is no cure as yet for the gradual and inevitable challenges of old age.

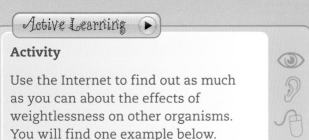

The effects of weightlessness on Salmonella bacteria

Research has been carried out on *Salmonella* bacteria in space. The zero gravity or micro gravity conditions experienced aboard the space shuttle while in the Earth's orbit have been shown to make these microbes much more infectious.

The *Salmonella* were carried into space and then given conditions in which they could grow. These bacteria are important in the study of human health and infection, as they are a major cause of food poisoning.

Weightlessness caused changes in the genes of these bacteria which resulted in the *Salmonella* becoming much more infectious. When compared with the *Salmonella* bacteria from the same culture that had been kept on Earth, the 'space' *Salmonella* that had been subjected to zero gravity had undergone changes to many of their genes. Back on Earth after the spaceflight, the bacteria were tested on animals. The results demonstrated that the *Salmonella* that had been in space were almost three times as likely to cause disease when compared with the control group of bacteria grown on Earth. It has been concluded that the forces encountered during spaceflight result in cells changing the manufacturing process of certain proteins.

Research undertaken on antibiotic resistance in *Salmonella* bacteria grown in zero gravity has found that a protective biofilm develops around the bacterium which is not seen to form around bacteria when grown on Earth. Biofilms are known to provide the bacteria with increased defence against the human immune system and antibiotics.

QUESTIONS

1 Create a memory map that summarises this short chapter. A memory map is a useful way of building the main points that you want to describe. It is as individual as the person who writes it. It is sometimes useful to have headings to start the process and we suggest the following:

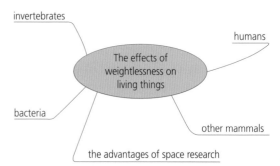

invertebrates

humans

The effects of weightlessness on living things

bacteria

other mammals

the advantages of space research

GLOSSARY

Astronaut American space adventurer

Cosmonaut Soviet space adventurer

FORCES, ELECTRICITY AND WAVES

Vibrations and Waves

6

From visible to beyond!

Level 2 — What came before?

 SCN 2-11b

By exploring reflections, the formation of shadows and the mixing of coloured lights, I can use my knowledge of the properties of light to show how it can be used in a creative way.

Level 3 — What is this chapter about?

 SCN 3-11b

By exploring radiations beyond the visible, I can describe a selected application, discussing the advantages and limitations.

From visible to beyond!

What is radiation?

Electromagnetic radiation is all around us. We are exposed to it every day in the water we drink, the food we eat and the air we breathe. Radiation travels through space and includes different energies such as heat and light, which we can feel or see. However, we cannot detect most radiation.

The Electromagnetic Spectrum

All forms of electromagnetic radiation are found on the Electromagnetic Spectrum. We rank the radiation in the **Electromagnetic Spectrum** from the lowest energy and highest wavelength to the highest energy and shortest wavelength. Each form of radiation in each part of the spectrum has a variety of different uses and dangers, depending on its wavelength and frequency. Radiation with the shortest wavelengths, higher frequencies and, therefore, most energy, presents the greatest hazards to living organisms.

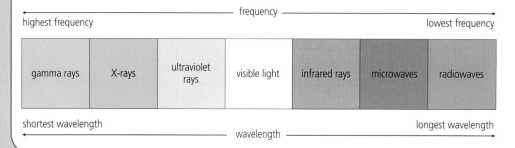

highest frequency ←————— frequency —————→ lowest frequency

| gamma rays | X-rays | ultraviolet rays | visible light | infrared rays | microwaves | radiowaves |

shortest wavelength ←————— wavelength —————→ longest wavelength

The visible spectrum

The visible spectrum lies between the infrared and ultraviolet part of the Electromagnetic Spectrum.

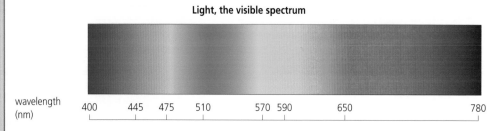

Light, the visible spectrum

wavelength (nm): 400   445   475   510   570 590   650   780

Each colour has a different wavelength. The shortest is violet with a wavelength of around 400 nanometres (nm) and the longest is red at around 700 nm.

Radiation and photosynthesis

Light energy from the sun is the driving force behind all life on Earth. Many living things – bacteria, algae and plants – can carry out photosynthesis.

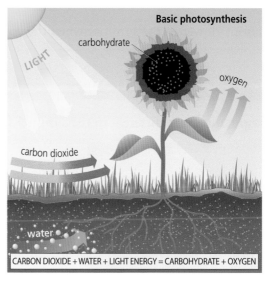

Basic photosynthesis

carbohydrate

LIGHT

oxygen

carbon dioxide

water

CARBON DIOXIDE + WATER + LIGHT ENERGY = CARBOHYDRATE + OXYGEN

Photosynthetic organisms range in size from microscopic algae to the largest trees such as the giant redwoods. They all trap the Sun's light energy to make their own food during photosynthesis.

Plant leaves contain the green **pigment** chlorophyll (pronounced klow-row-fill). Chlorophyll is arguably one of the most important chemicals on the planet since it is able to trap light energy, which is then converted into chemical energy. Of the visible spectrum, red and blue light are the most useful source of energy for photosynthesis, and as a result chlorophyll mostly absorbs light at these wavelengths.

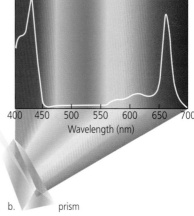

Chlorophyll absorption spectrum of visible light

Wavelength (nm)

400 450 500 550 600 650 700

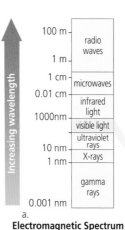

Increasing wavelength

100 m — radio waves
1 m
1 cm — microwaves
0.01 cm
1000nm — infrared light
— visible light
— ultraviolet rays
10 nm
1 nm — X-rays
— gamma rays
0.001 nm

a.
Electromagnetic Spectrum

b.   prism

What happens to the remaining light?

Red and blue light is absorbed. Green light passes through the plant or is reflected and as a result the leaves appear green in colour. But those wavelengths still contain energy. Plants contain additional pigments which help them absorb light from additional parts of the spectrum. This explains why not all plants are green.

Flowering

Poinsettia plants are popular Christmas decorations but they do not flower naturally until the spring, after a period of short days. **Horticulturalists** give them artificial long, dark nights for around two months in autumn to force them to produce flowers at Christmas.

Carnations flower in the summer when the days are longer.

Seasonal migration

Bird populations are different in the summer from the winter.

British swallows spend the winter in southern Africa. They fly 10 000 km twice a year!

Barnacle geese spend the summer in the arctic. They fly 1700 km twice a year!

These bird migrations are signalled by changing day-length in the spring or in the autumn.

Phototaxis

Phototaxis is the movement of living things in response to light.

Microscopic living things are often able to swim towards the light and carry out photosynthesis.

Brine shrimps, sometimes called sea monkeys, feed on algae. Brine shrimps swim towards the light to collect their food.

Medical applications of the visible spectrum

Visible light can be used as a treatment for several disorders, especially **jaundice** in newborn babies. A Danish Scientist called Niels Ryberg Finsen received the **Nobel Prize** for Physiology or Medicine in 1903, for his use of light in the treatment of skin diseases.

Newborn babies born with jaundice have waste materials in their blood from when they were in the womb. The signs of jaundice are yellow skin and eyes. Jaundice is treated by exposing the baby to intense light for 12–14 hours. Light absorbed by the skin helps the body breakdown and remove the waste materials.

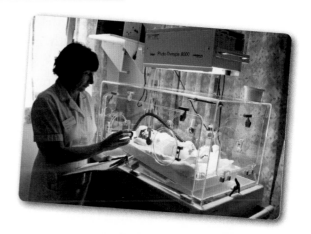

Lasers

Lasers have been used in surgery since the 1960s and are used in lots of different ways. The heat from a laser beam can help surgeons to carry out very precise operations. They are commonly used because they can cut tissue with minimum damage and bleeding.

Lasers are often used on skin for cosmetic reasons e.g. to remove birthmarks, tattoos and wrinkles.

Lasers, attached to fibre-optic probes, allow surgeons to carry out operations that previously required major surgery and long periods in hospital. Routine operations are carried out on eyes, kidneys and the heart – micro-lasers are used to reopen blocked arteries, or seal blood vessels to prevent bleeding.

QUESTIONS

1 Prepare four questions to research the effects of light on plants and animals.

2 Chlorophyll is green. Why do the leaves of some plants appear different colours, such as red?

3 Find out about other substances that are present in plants. Explain the benefits to plants of having these substances.

Applications beyond the visible spectrum

Electromagnetic radiation exists beyond the visible spectrum; some with longer wavelengths (and lower energies) than visible light e.g. infrared rays, microwaves, and radio waves, and those with shorter wavelengths (and higher energies) than visible light, e.g. ultraviolet rays, X-rays and gamma rays.

Infrared radiation (IR)

Infrared heat or thermal radiation is released when something moves. The hotter an object, the more infrared radiation is produced.

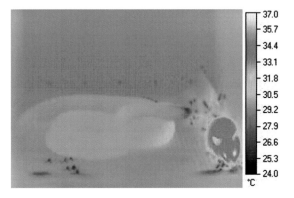

Although you cannot see infrared radiation you can feel it as heat. You are sensitive to temperature, because the nerve endings in your skin detect infrared radiation. All animals emit infrared radiation and we can determine the hottest regions of an animal's body by studying thermal images of them.

Some animals, for example snakes from the pit viper family, such as rattlesnakes, can detect infrared with their sensory pits. This adaptation helps them detect their prey even in the dark.

The mouse in this image is emitting infrared rediation that the rattlesnake can detect – even in the dark.

Night vision

Soldiers use IR kit to spot other soldiers at night.

Scientists observe animals during the night using infrared cameras. This has led to a greater understanding of **nocturnal** behaviour in many animals.

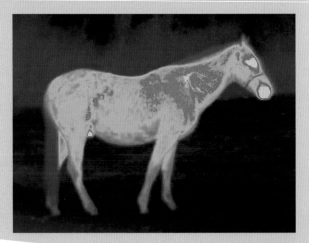

Medical uses of IR

Infrared cameras are used to help with cancer screening. This technology is called **thermography**.

Cancer is abnormal growth of cells in the body. Rapidly growing cancers give off more heat than that of normal tissue and this can be detected with an IR camera. Early detection of this kind reduces the need for surgery or radiation therapy.

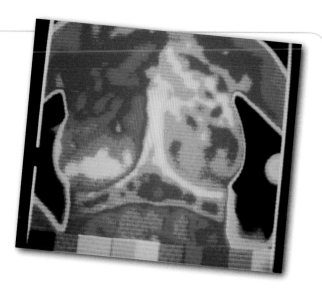

Microwaves

Microwaves have a lower frequency and longer wavelength than visible light on the Electromagnetic Spectrum.

The most common medical use of microwave radiation has been for warming internal parts of the body, using a technique called **diathermy**. This can help relieve muscle soreness, treat inflammation, seal wounds to stop them bleeding and even help kill cancer cells.

Radio waves

Radio waves have lower frequencies than microwaves and the longest wavelengths of the Electromagnetic Spectrum.

The water in food absorbs microwaves and this causes the food to heat up and cook. The heat will damage or kill the cells. Microwaves also have many medical uses.

Televisions, radios, wireless telephones and even remote car keys use radio waves.

From visible to beyond!

Imaging

Magnetic Resonance Imaging (**MRI**) scans are routinely used to create images of the body's internal organs. MRI uses strong magnetic fields and radio waves to build up detailed pictures of a cross-section of the body and its organs.

By combining the pictures from several scans, doctors can build up three-dimensional images, which can be displayed on a computer screen for immediate diagnosis of certain cancers and diseases.

Ultraviolet rays

Ultraviolet (UV) rays are located between visible light and X-rays on the electromagnetic spectrum. UV is naturally found in sunlight. Sunburn is caused by being over-exposed to UV.

Other animals such as bees, some birds, reptiles and fish can detect UV light and often use it for navigation, to find a mate or locate food.

Forensic scientists use UV radiation and a chemical called luminol to highlight body fluids e.g. blood at crime scenes. Fake blood was used here.

Some skin disorders can be detected with UV light; exposing skin to UV radiation can treat other conditions such as acne.

!Health warning! UV must be used carefully. High energy UV can damage the DNA in our cells and is **the** major cause of skin cancer. UV can also damage parts of the eye; in particular, the retina, lens and cornea, so eye protection should be worn when you are exposed to UV radiation.

X-rays

X-rays have shorter wavelengths and, therefore, higher energy than ultraviolet waves. We cannot see or feel X-rays. They do pass through our skin and soft tissue but cannot pass through bone very well.

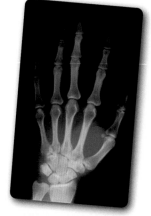

You might have had an X-ray taken in a hospital or clinic to find out if you have broken or fractured a bone. Doctors have diagnosed broken bones with X-rays since the late nineteenth century. The X-rays pass through the body tissues, but are partly absorbed by the bones. This casts a shadow and an image is formed on a digital detector.

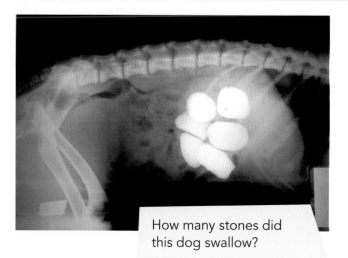

How many stones did this dog swallow?

A **CAT** (computerised axial tomographic) **scan** or more commonly known as a CT scan can build a detailed picture of the body. CT scans are a series of **X-ray** images taken from different angles to create cross-sectional images of the body. These detailed images help doctors investigate signs of disease and cancer.

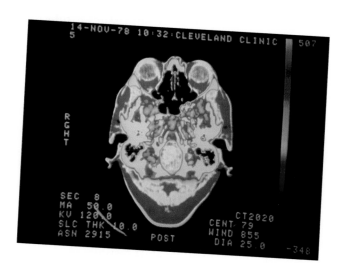

! Health warning! Even low doses of X-rays can damage the DNA in cells and cause cancer. Precautions are taken in hospitals to limit the dose of X-ray radiation received by patients and staff. **Radiographers** are protected and stand behind lead screens to reduce the level of radiation to which they are exposed.

Gamma rays

Gamma waves have a very high frequency, the shortest wavelengths, and the most energy of any other radiation in the Electromagnetic Spectrum. We cannot see or feel **gamma rays** but they can pass through our skin and soft tissue and our cells can even absorb some rays.

Gamma rays have a number of useful applications in a variety of industries from medicine and food, to plastics and sewage treatment.

Gamma rays can kill living cells. Exposure to controlled doses of gamma radiation can help kill cancer cells. Gamma rays are used to sterilise surgical instruments and other medical supplies. They can also be used in the food processing industry to kill harmful bacteria in food. This can reduce the need for chemical preservatives in food. Gamma rays are also useful in the treatment of sewage and water purification due to their ability to kill disease-causing organisms (pathogens).

! Health warning! Despite their useful properties, unnecessary or over-exposure to gamma rays can increase the risk of damage to cells and can lead to cancer. Exposure to such types of radiation should be carefully restricted to reduce any potential health risks.

Summary

Electromagnetic radiation, both in the visible and non-visible spectrum offers humans many opportunities. Our life and culture is dependent on it in one form or another. Many of our most exciting medical and communication technologies depend on electromagnetic radiation. In fact, all living organisms are totally dependent on electromagnetic radiation in the form of solar energy from the Sun. It is the driving force behind all food chains on Earth and has over many millions of years been responsible for the creation of fossil fuels, currently the major global source of all fuel. Our ability to appreciate the visual beauty of the world around us depends on the sensitivity of our eyes to the visible light part of the spectrum, without which we could not see. The applications of the Electromagnetic Spectrum are clear to see and no doubt there will be many more discoveries in the future that will further enhance our understanding and use of it. Despite the expansive range of technologies on offer, our use of them should nonetheless be tempered with caution, as high doses of radiation can be hazardous to life.

QUESTIONS

1 Prepare a memory map to summarise the ways in which electromagnetic radiation is used for medical diagnosis today.

2 Find out more about lasers in disciplines other than medicine e.g. engineering and the military.

3 What health risks are brought about by the use of lasers?

4 Thermographs are used to detect infrared radiation. Explain the differences between the mouse and the snake on page 64.

GLOSSARY

CAT scan a three-dimensional X-ray image formed by a computer

Diathermy electromagnetically produced heat that can be used as a form of therapy

Electromagnetic radiation radiation that is made up from waves

Electromagnetic Spectrum the whole range of electromagnetic radiation

Forensic using science for legal purposes

Gamma ray high energy, short wave, electromagnetic radiation

Horticulture science of plant cultivation

Jaundice symptom of diseases of the liver where the white of the eye and the skin may appear yellow

Laser narrow concentrated beam of light

MRI medical imaging technique that relies on powerful magnetic fields to provide detailed knowledge of soft tissues inside the body

Nobel Prize annual award for the most outstanding global contribution to physics, chemistry, physiology and medicine

Nocturnal animals active at night

Phototaxis movement of living things in response to light

Pigment a coloured chemical

Radiographer hospital staff responsible for taking the X-ray, MRI images etc.

Thermography technique for detecting heat sources

Ultraviolet rays invisible radiation that comes from the sun

X-rays high energy invisible electromagnetic radiation

BIOLOGICAL SYSTEMS
Body Systems and Cells

Introducing biological systems

Level 2   What came before?

 SCN 2-07a

By investigating how friction, including air resistance, affects motion, I can suggest ways to improve efficiency in moving objects.

 SCN 2-10a

To begin to understand how batteries work, I can help to build simple chemical cells using readily-available materials which can be used to make an appliance work.

 SCN 2-12a

By investigating some body systems and potential problems which they may develop, I can make informed decisions to help me to maintain my health and wellbeing.

Level 3   What is this chapter about?

 SCN 3-12a

I have explored the structure and function of organs and organ systems and can relate this to the basic biological processes required to sustain life.

 SCN 3-07a

By contributing to investigations of energy loss due to friction, I can suggest ways of improving the efficiency of moving systems.

 SCN 3-10a

I can help to design simple chemical cells and use them to investigate the factors which affect the voltage produced.

Introducing biological systems

A modern car includes several 'systems' which allows it to run and make sure that it is safe, efficient and comfortable.

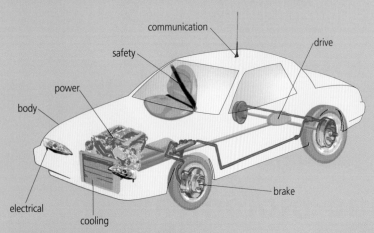

Body system

A car's body is designed to improve performance by reducing 'drag', the friction of the car moving against the air. The designers also use the body to improve waterproofing and soundproofing, as well as trying to make it look good.

Drive system

Pistons, gears and drive shafts transfer the kinetic energy from the engine to the wheels, making the car move.

Brake system

The brakes rely on **hydraulic** fluid to push pads on to the wheel discs and slow the car down. Brake pads and discs can become very hot due to friction.

Cooling system

When fuel burns in the engine it releases a lot of heat. Each car must remove that heat otherwise the engine will 'seize' and moving parts will fuse together. The radiator takes air across a cooling fluid to remove that extra heat.

Electrical system

Electricity is used in many ways to make the car work. Electrical sparks inside the engine cause the fuel to explode to start things moving. Think of all the equipment in a car that relies on electricity e.g. lights, instrument display, heating, locking, entertainment and navigation.

Technological systems

The modern car relies on sensors and onboard computers to communicate how well the car is performing. These make sure that the engine is performing properly. Airbags are controlled by computers in the car. Many cars are also able to use satellite navigation systems.

Power system

The engine allows other parts of the car to work. Engines are usually fuelled by petrol or diesel. 'Hybrid' cars are becoming more common and use petrol, diesel and electricity. We may see hydrogen being used in the near future.

Safety system

'**Crumple zones**', seat belts, shatterproof wind screens, disc brakes, modern tyres, and air bags make the car safer for drivers and passengers. Lights and horns help to alert other road users and pedestrians that they are in danger.

A car cannot work properly unless all of the systems are working well. Each system needs to be properly maintained.

Our body is the same and is made up of several systems that depend on each other and contribute to our health and well being.

Something about the skeletal system

What does it do?
The skeleton supports and protects you.

What is in it?
The skeletal system includes bones, ligaments and tendons.

What other systems does it work with?
Muscles move the skeleton in two different positions allowing you to move.

Large hollow bones e.g. the hip and the long leg bones contain marrow which makes red (cardiovascular) and white (immune) blood cells.

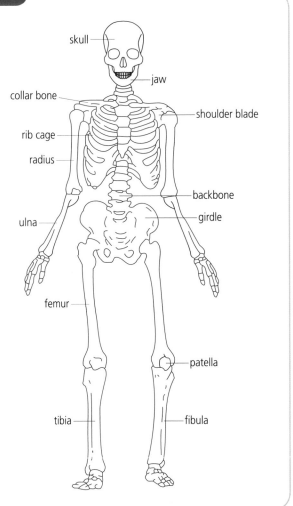

skull

jaw

collar bone

shoulder blade

rib cage

radius

backbone

girdle

ulna

femur

patella

tibia

fibula

Something about the respiratory system

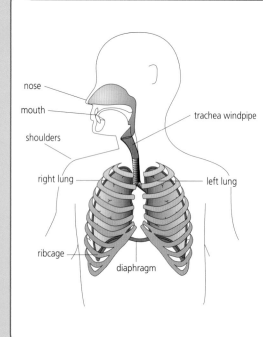

What does it do?

The respiratory system allows you to breathe.

What is in it?

The respiratory system includes your nose, mouth and windpipe. This system carries air in and out of your lungs. The respiratory system also includes the muscles that surround your lungs – the diaphragm on the chest floor and the shoulders and ribs that surround it.

What other systems does it work with?

The respiratory system helps oxygen to enter your bloodstream as well as removing carbon dioxide from your lungs (carbon dioxide removal is essential to prevent the blood **pH** changing). The muscular system makes the chest move air in and out of the lungs. The skeleton protects the chest.

Something about the digestive system

What does it do?

The digestive system breaks insoluble food into soluble **nutrients**. Your teeth, stomach and intestines break the food into tiny pieces (mechanical breakdown) so that acid in the stomach and enzymes throughout the system can complete the process (chemical breakdown).

What is in it?

The digestive system includes the mouth, oesophagus, stomach, liver, pancreas and intestines.

What other systems does it work with?

Most nutrients pass into the bloodstream (cardiovascular system) but digested fats and oils pass into the lymphatic system. The muscular system moves food through the entire digestive system. (It is this movement that causes the sound that is made when your stomach rumbles!)

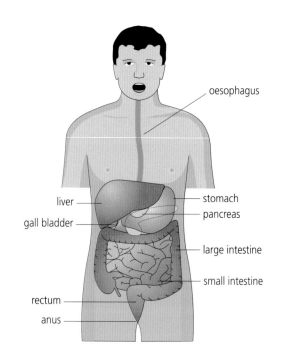

Something about the muscular system

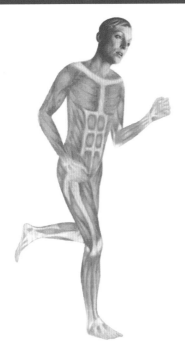

What is in it?

You have three kinds of muscle in your body.

Skeletal muscle lets you move from place to place when you want to. The muscle which is found inside your body cannot be controlled and works automatically. It looks different under the microscope. Your heart is made from the third kind of muscle – **cardiac**.

What other systems does it work with?

Muscles work with the skeletal system, the digestive system and the cardiovascular system. They are controlled by the nervous system.

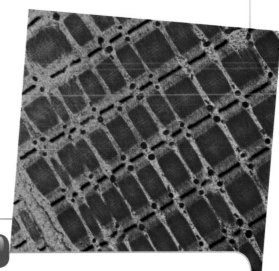

What does it do?

The muscular system makes your body move. It moves materials inside your body as well.

Something about the lymphatic system

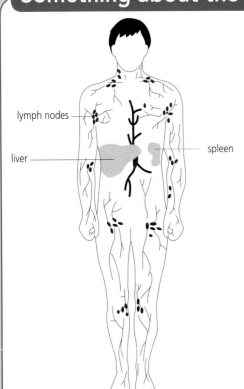

lymph nodes

liver

spleen

What does it do?

The lymphatic system helps to drain fluid through your body, transports digested oil and fat, **lipids**, and helps to protect you from diseases.

What is in it?

Lymph vessels return body fluids to the heart and then around the body. Lymph nodes, the lumps that you sometimes feel below your jaw when you have a sore throat, filter germs from your body. The lymphatic system also makes **antibodies**, chemicals which protect you from diseases. The BCG vaccine helps you make antibodies which attack the tuberculosis germ. The HPV vaccine helps girls make antibodies which protect them from cervical cancer.

What other systems does it work with?

The lymphatic system works with the digestive system and the immune system.

Something about the endocrine system

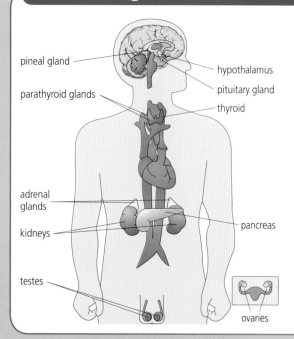

pineal gland
hypothalamus
pituitary gland
parathyroid glands
thyroid
adrenal glands
kidneys
pancreas
testes
ovaries

What does it do?

The **endocrine** system sends **hormones** around your body.

What is in it?

The endocrine system includes glands which release **hormones**. Hormones travel through the bloodstream. They usually have their effect on another part of the body. Hormones released from the pituitary gland change the way that other endocrine glands are working. The pituitary gland is often called the 'master gland'.

What other systems does it work with?

The endocrine system works the cardiovascular system and the nervous system.

Something about the cardiovascular system

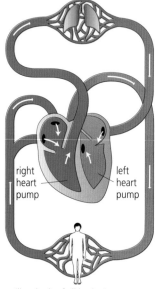

capillary beds of lungs, gas exchange occurs here

right heart pump

left heart pump

capillary beds of all body tissues except lungs, gas exchange occurs here

oxygen-poor blood   oxygen-rich blood

What does it do?

The **cardiovascular** system transports blood throughout your body. Your blood carries food, heat, oxygen and hormones everywhere in your body. It also removes waste materials e.g. carbon dioxide.

What is in it?

The cardiovascular system includes the heart, a powerful pump, which forces blood through pipes called **arteries, capillaries** and **veins**. Arteries carry blood away from the heart at high pressure. Capillaries are tiny and carry blood through all your organs. Veins return blood to the heart at low pressure and these also have valves to keep your blood flowing in the correct direction.

What other systems does it work with?

The cardiovascular system works with all other body systems. The speed it works at is controlled by the nervous and the endocrine systems.

Capillaries in your face carry blood to the surface when you need to lose heat or when you are embarrassed.

Something about the reproductive system

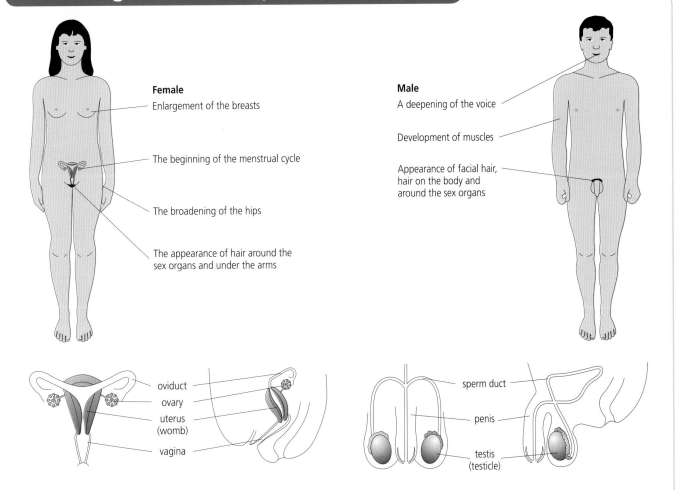

Female
— Enlargement of the breasts

— The beginning of the menstrual cycle

— The broadening of the hips

— The appearance of hair around the sex organs and under the arms

Male
— A deepening of the voice

— Development of muscles

— Appearance of facial hair, hair on the body and around the sex organs

oviduct
ovary
uterus (womb)
vagina

sperm duct
penis
testis (testicle)

What does it do?

The reproductive system allows you to have children. Girls make eggs (ova). Boys make **sperm**. **Ova** are fertilised by sperm after sexual intercourse has taken place. Once fertilisation has taken place a baby will grow inside the mother during the next nine months.

What is in it?

The reproductive system includes the sex organs. Girls – your sex organs include the ovaries and the womb. Boys – your sex organs include the testes and the penis.

During **puberty** your bodies change and you become young men and women. Girls' body shape changes during puberty. Breast development and the start of periods take place at this time. Boys' body shape also changes. Your voice becomes deeper and growth is often rapid.

What other systems does it work with?

The reproductive system works with the cardiovascular system, the nervous system and the endocrine system.

Something about the urinary system

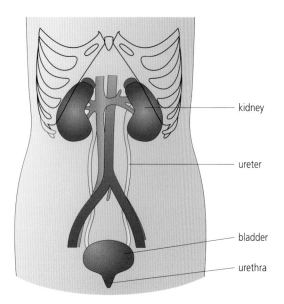

kidney

ureter

bladder

urethra

urea are dissolved in the blood, removed by your kidneys and pass out of the body in the **urine**.

What is in it?

The urinary system has four main parts. Your kidneys clean the blood and make urine which is sent to the bladder for storage through pipes called ureters. You empty your bladder each time you go to the bathroom.

What other systems does it work with?

The urinary system works with the cardiovascular and endocrine systems in particular. The kidneys have a rich blood supply and hormones control the volume of urine that you release depending on how much water is in your bloodstream.

What does it do?

The urinary system purifies your blood and allows you to remove waste from your body. Salts and

Something about the immune system

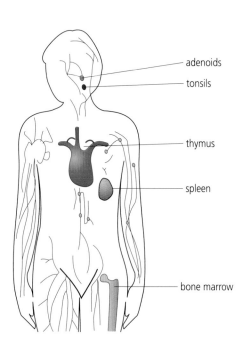

adenoids

tonsils

thymus

spleen

bone marrow

What does it do?

The immune system protects you against diseases. It does this by making antibodies, white blood cells and by filtering germs from your blood and lymph.

What is in it?

The immune system includes several organs which defend you against disease. These organs make antibodies. These often stick germs together. Organs in the immune system also make white blood cells which attack germs and foreign materials.

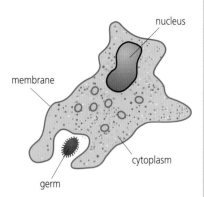

nucleus

membrane

cytoplasm

germ

What other systems does it work with?

The immune system depends on the skeletal system; stem cells are made in red marrow. White cells and antibodies are found throughout the cardiovascular and lymphatic systems.

Something about the body surface system

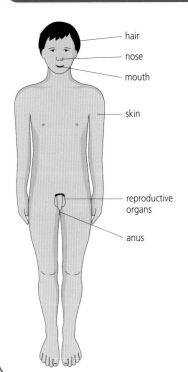

hair
nose
mouth
skin
reproductive organs
anus

What does it do?

Your body is covered with skin. Skin helps to control your temperature – we sweat when we are hot and shiver when we are cold. It is waterproof which means that germs can be washed off. Salt and other chemicals in sweat kill germs.

Mucus covers the surface of your mouth, nose, reproductive organs and anus. Mucus contains chemicals that trap and destroy germs

What is in it?

The body surface system includes the skin, hair and body openings.

What other systems does it work with?

The body surface system works with the cardiovascular system and it responds to the nervous system e.g. when you blush. The endocrine system can make you turn white when you are frightened.

Something about the nervous system

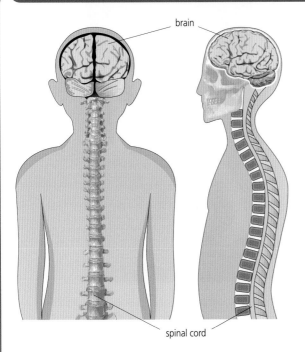

brain

spinal cord

What does it do?

Your nervous system is a communication system which collects and transfers nervous information around your body and brain. It is really an electrical system which connects every part of your body and brain.

What is in it?

The central nervous system is made up of your brain and spinal cord. The central nervous system connects the sense organs e.g. eyes, ears, skin and nose, to your brain. This makes you aware of everything around you. We also have nerves that are not directly connected to the brain so that automatic responses – reflexes – take place.

What other systems does it work with?

The nervous system works with the other systems in lots of different ways. The skeletal system protects your ears and eyes. The nervous system controls heart and breathing rate.

QUESTIONS

1 Name the main organs or tissues that are found in each of the following systems:

   a) skeletal

   b) respiratory

   c) digestive

   d) urinary

   e) nervous.

2 Write a short note to explain how:

   a) the muscular system helps the digestive system

   b) the immune system makes use of the circulatory system

   c) the skeletal system works with the muscular system.

3 Prepare a display on one of the body systems.

Skeletal movement

Human **kinetics**, sometimes called **kinesiology**, is the science of human movement.

Here are two reasons why scientists analyse movement.

Assist recovery from injuries.

Improve performance of sports men and women.

Powerful computers and three-dimensional video systems are often used to record people's movement.

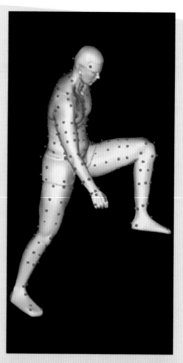

Reflective markers that are placed around the body enable a computer record to be made of the movement. This allows greater analysis to be made and lead to improved recovery.

The same technology is used for entertainment purposes – actors' movements are used to create animated characters for movies and computer games.

Research is also carried out into the way that clothing and footwear affects our movement.

Movement and friction

You can move from place to place because your muscles move your skeleton into different positions. Each joint is a source of a possible friction. Movable joints are designed to reduce friction and to protect you from damage due to the impact caused as you move around.

Sometimes our joints can become a painful. They can become swollen after knocks, bumps or twists. You usually recover quickly from such injuries. First aid recommends rest, ice and elevation to assist speedy recovery.

Arthritis refers to any condition when a joint is painful. There are more than 100 diseases or conditions that can affect your joints.

Although arthritis can affect you at any age the majority of cases occur in adults.

- More than one-third of the population aged over 50 have arthritic pain.

- More than 10 million adults (6 million women and 4 million men) consult their GP each year with arthritis and related conditions.

- More than 6 million people in the UK have painful **osteoarthritis** in one or both knees.

- More than 650 000 in the UK have painful osteoarthritis in one or both hips.

- More than 1 million adults consult their GP each year with osteoarthritis.

- In Scotland over 6000 hip replacements and 6300 knee replacements were performed in one year.

- 10 million working days were lost in one year as a result of these conditions.

(The Arthritis Research Campaign)

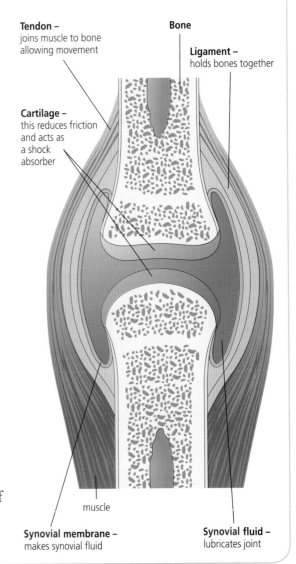

Tendon – joins muscle to bone allowing movement

Bone

Ligament – holds bones together

Cartilage – this reduces friction and acts as a shock absorber

muscle

Synovial membrane – makes synovial fluid

Synovial fluid – lubricates joint

QUESTIONS

1 Find out more about either:

   a) the use of computers to improve sport performance

   b) the use of computers to improve physical disability.

2 Construct a model of a joint from everyday materials. Include in the model:

   a) bones

   b) muscles

   c) tendons

   d) ligaments

   e) cartilage

   f) synovial membrane.

Living things make and use electricity too!

In 1818, Matthew Clydesdale, a weaver from the Airdrie area, was found guilty of murder and on the 3rd of October he was 'hung and anatomised'. This meant that after execution he would be **dissected** by anatomy professors at the University of Glasgow.

The anatomists repeated **Galvani's** experiments with frogs and attached a battery through metal conductors to various parts of Clydesdale's body. They could make his knee bend, or create breathing movements in the chest or even change the expressions on his face!

All living things make electricity. Each **living cell** in many ways resembles the **electrical cell** that you put into your appliances.

Cells concentrate some chemicals inside and prevent the entry of other ones. Although these differences only create tiny voltages across the cell membrane they have a huge effect on the way that the cell is able to work.

Le docteur Ure galvanisant le corps de l'assassin Clydesdale. (Doctor Ure galvanising the body of the murderer Clydesdale.)

Although most cells generate tiny voltages the electric eel can create currents of 1 ampere at between 600 and 1000 volts which it uses to stun its prey or to defend it from predators.

Nerve cells

Nerve cells stretch through every part of your body. When you stretch your arm your brain sends messages through your body to the arm muscles and makes them move.

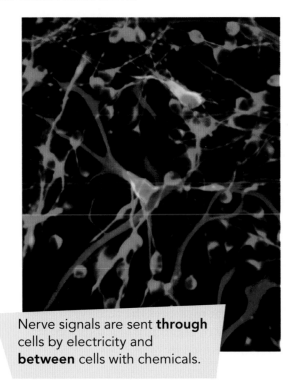

Nerve signals are sent **through** cells by electricity and **between** cells with chemicals.

Scientists are very interested in everything to do with electricity and living things.

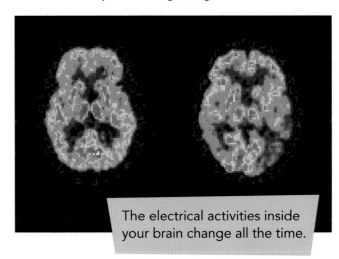

The electrical activities inside your brain change all the time.

QUESTIONS

1 📖 Find out more about one of the following:

a) the 'Edinburgh Body Snatchers'

b) science and the Scottish Enlightenment

c) electrical animals

d) electricity and diagnosis

e) electricity and therapy.

GLOSSARY

Antibody Y-shaped protein part of the immune system

Artery blood vessel that carries blood away from the heart

Arthritis joint inflammation

Capillary tiniest blood vessel that takes blood into and away from the body tissues

Cardiac (Adjective) relating to the heart

Cardiovascular (Adjective) relating to the circulatory system – the heart and the blood vessels

Cartilage elastic connective tissue that covers the ends of bones

Crumple zone part of a vehicle which is designed to collapse and absorb the energy during a crash

Dissect to cut and examine closely

Electrical cell a device that is capable of changing chemical energy into electricity

Endocrine (Adjective) relating to the glands which secrete hormones into the blood

Hormone hormones are chemicals that the body makes to control several processes in the body

Hydraulic moved by water or other liquids

Kinesiology the science of human movement

Kinetics branch of mechanics that deals with forces and movement

Lipid chemical group that includes fats and oils

Living cell the cell is the basic building block of all living things

Luigi Galvani (1737–1798) an Italian scientist who discovered that electricity can be brought about by chemical reactions

Lymph tissue fluid which is returned to the circulation in lymph vessels

Mucus protective liquid found in the mouth, nose and other body openings

Nutrient a substance which may provide nourishment – may be organic or inorganic

Ova (Plural) (Singular ovum) unfertilised eggs – female sex cells

pH scale that measures the acidity, neutrality or alkalinity of a solution ranging from 0 to 14

Puberty stage of development when an individual becomes sexually mature

Sperm male sex cells

Synovial lubricating fluid inside the joints

Urea poisonous chemical that is made in the liver and passes out of the body in the urine

Vein blood vessel that carries blood towards the heart

BIOLOGICAL SYSTEMS

Body Systems and Cells

8

What is technology and what is health?

Level 2 — What came before?

 SCN2-12b

I have explored the structure and function of sensory organs to develop my understanding of body actions in response to outside conditions.

Level 3 — What is this chapter about?

 SCN3-12b

I have explored the role of technology in monitoring health and improving the quality of life.

What is technology and what is health?

Here are two statements for you to think about:

'Technology is ... the know-how and creative processes that may assist people to utilise tools, resources and systems to solve problems and to enhance control over the natural and made environment in an endeavour to improve the human condition' (**UNESCO** 1985).

'Health is a state of complete physical, mental and social well-being and not merely the absence of disease or infirmity '(**WHO** 1948).

United Nations Educational, Scientific and Cultural Organization

When we feel unwell our body changes:

You feel warmer

You cough and sneeze

Your pulse rate quickens

You feel sore and uncomfortable

You recognise these **symptoms** and technology can help these observations so you can make an accurate **diagnosis.**

Many different diagnostic tools exist to help monitor the state of your health and detect any health problems even before we may feel any symptoms of ill health. Doctors use these tools to build up a picture of your health and discover medical conditions. This allows them to take steps to improve your health by encouraging you to lead a more healthy life e.g. through taking regular exercise, eating a balanced diet, cutting down on fat and salt in your diet and avoiding certain foods.

Think!

Think about the times you have visited your doctor. What types of equipment or technology did your doctor use to monitor your health? Make a list and beside each describe what you think they monitor.

Heart rate

When you feel your pulse on your wrist or neck you are feeling the effect of blood being forced through your arteries.

Pulse measurement in the wrist

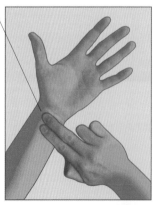

It is more accurate, however, to use a pulse monitor.

Heart rate

One of the most commonly used pieces of equipment, the **stethoscope**, was designed in 1816 by a French doctor and is used for listening to the sounds of the body's internal organs; in particular, those of the heart.

Try listening to your own heartbeat or that of a classmate using a stethoscope in the laboratory. Describe what you hear. Try counting the number of times you heart beats in one minute. Listen to your belly as well.

The adult heart rate, while resting, normally ranges from 60 to 100 beats per minute. Athletes can have a very slow heart rate because their training exercises the heart muscle. Your heart rate will change depending on factors such as activity, fitness, body position and emotions.

A doctor can **diagnose** an abnormal heart rate with a stethoscope. They can then carry out further tests or prescribe medicine.

Blood pressure

Blood pressure (**BP**) is a measure of the force of the blood flowing through blood vessels after a heartbeat. The tool, which is used to assess BP and provide an idea of the health of the heart, and the circulatory system, is called a **sphygmomanometer** (pronounced Sfig-mow-man-om-meter). (Most people call it a 'sfig' because it is such a hard word to say!)

BP changes after each beat of the heart as it contracts and relaxes. The *maximum* pressure is shown as the upper reading and the *minimum* pressure is shown in the lower reading. A 'normal' blood pressure reading for a 20 year old is 120/70. Blood pressure changes as you get older.

High or low blood pressure may cause a doctor concern, and could result in the patient being advised to make a change to their diet or perhaps take medication to bring their blood pressure back to a safe/healthy reading.

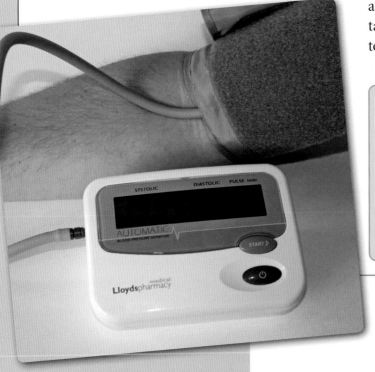

Active Learning ▶

Activity

👍 Find out what type of blood pressure monitoring kits you have in school and have a go at measuring your own blood pressure. What factors do you think will affect your blood pressure?

Rhythm of the heart

The health of the heart rhythm can be assessed in hospital using an **electrocardiogram** (ECG) (pronounced electro-cardio-gram). The ECG allows the electrical currents that travel from the heart through the body to be detected and recorded.

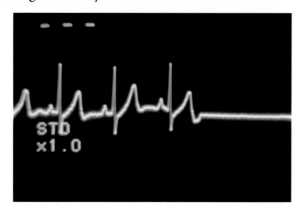

An abnormal ECG can indicate that the heart is not beating with a regular rhythm and may indicate that a heart attack has been experienced.

Using this range of technologies, the health of our hearts can be examined. Information gained can be used to offer people the opportunity to make changes to their lifestyle in order to look after their hearts.

'Defib'

During a heart attack and other serious conditions, the heart stops beating, or beats in an irregular way. A controlled electrical shock with a **defibrillator** can restore the normal heart rhythm.

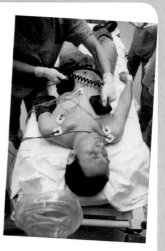

Active Learning

Activity

Currently, heart disease is one of the leading causes of death in Scotland, particularly in the west of the country. Try to find out the major causes of heart disease and why it is that there should be a higher incidence in this part of the country. What advice would you offer people to best look after their hearts?

Endoscopes

X-rays and other technologies enable diagnosis of damage to bones. Soft tissues do not show up well on X-rays and doctors could not make an accurate diagnosis of many conditions without surgically opening up a person.

Now with the **endoscope**, it is possible for doctors to look inside our bodies. We can investigate the internal health of our organs such as the stomach or intestines by feeding a flexible tube with a light source and tiny camera to take photographs of the insides of the organs. Any abnormalities, such as stomach ulcers, can show up without the need of invasive surgery and has again allowed early diagnosis of potential problems, such as cancer.

Advances to endoscope technology have resulted in the development and widespread use of

Endoscopes

endoscopes for key-hole surgery. Endoscopes for this purpose have surgical instruments attached, which can be remotely controlled by the doctor carrying out the key-hole surgery. Samples of tissues and organs can also be retrieved in this way (biopsy) to be analysed for signs of disease.

Endoscopes and key-hole surgery allow access to our internal organs and this has reduced the need for surgery. This helps to speed up patients' recovery.

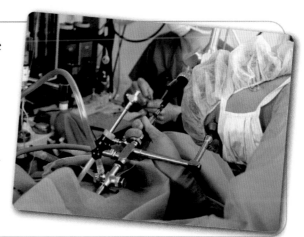

Blood testing

Doctors may take blood samples from patients and run various diagnostic tests to assess a number of factors such as red and white blood cell counts, confirmation of blood groups, protein/glucose levels, presence of antibodies and saturation of oxygen etc. The presence or lack of these substances helps doctors diagnose infections and potential health disorders.

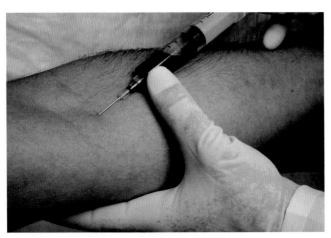

Diagnostic tools have life-saving potential. They can allow early detection of medical conditions and offer people the opportunity to make changes to their lifestyle, or take medication which can help improve the quality of their life and help them live longer and healthier lives.

Blood-glucose monitoring kits are small test kits that can be easily carried around and allow

diabetics to monitor the glucose levels in their body, at any time of day. A convenient and easy test to use, it involves the sufferer pricking the skin to obtain a small sample of blood and placing it on a small test strip of paper. The test strip is then inserted into the glucose test kit, which will give a numerical blood glucose reading within about five seconds. Technology such as this can help people take responsibility for and care for their own health and establish how regularly they need to take their medication. If the blood glucose reading is too low it can indicate the need to eat food, or if it is too high, the need to adjust the dosage of insulin, a drug which reduces blood glucose levels. Sufferers can, therefore, lead more independent lives and ensure their blood glucose levels are maintained at acceptable limits. In the long run this can also reduce the risk of diabetes-related complications, such as damage to the eyes and nerves.

Peak flow

Technology also helps people living with conditions such as asthma or diabetes to monitor and manage their condition and use of medication. The **peak flow** meter helps asthmatics keep an eye on the severity of their asthma.

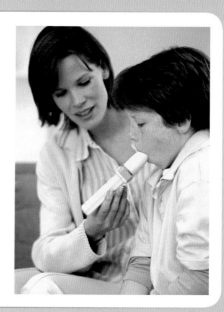

This simple piece of technology measures the rate at which air can be forced out of the lungs and is measured in litres per minute. By measuring their peak flow and comparing it with normal readings for someone of that age, sex and height, asthmatics can assess how well their lungs are working and how effective their medication is in treating their condition. Technologists design the best inhalers and the best ways of delivering the medication, through suitably sized particles for maximum uptake in the lungs.

Obesity – a growing problem

The development and advancement of medical technology has generated a huge level of public interest in health. You only have to look in the newspapers, on the Internet and watch the news on television to see the widespread reporting of health.

One of the major health concerns at the moment is the rising cases of **obesity** in the UK. In fact, it is currently estimated that a quarter of the population is obese, and this figure appears likely to rise. How can we monitor and tackle this problem? One of the simplest technologies that we can use to measure our body mass is, of course, the bathroom scales. It is also possible to measure our percentage of body fat using a low-tech method such as skin fold callipers.

More advanced methods include a body fat sensor. This looks like bathroom scales but it sends a weak electric current through the body. It provides us with an instant measure of the percentage of body fat. This technology is now widely available and can be found in certain pharmacies throughout the UK. It is clear that people have become much more aware of the need to adopt a healthier

lifestyle, and the availability of technologies such as body fat sensors allow us to make informed judgements about the health of our bodies. By recognising the healthy limits of our bodies, this gives us the opportunity to make changes to our diet and lifestyle and improve the quality of our lives.

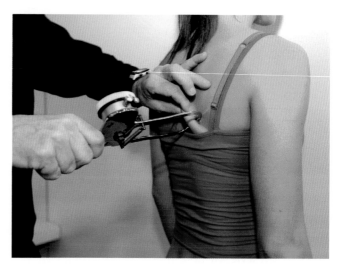

Active Learning ▶

Activities

1. 👍 Think about a disease that you have suffered.

   a) How did you feel when you were ill?

   b) Explain what you would do to diagnose if somebody else was suffering these symptoms.

   c) Describe what you would do to make them feel better.

2. 👍 Find out about government health priorities. Imagine that these had been announced today. Write your report in the style of a newspaper article.

Radiation protection

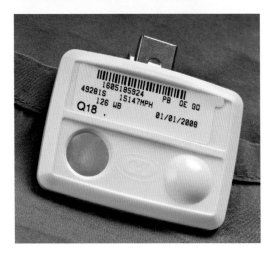

Radiation is dangerous to human health. It can cause damage to the DNA in our body cells, increasing the risk of cancers, and at high doses can completely kill the cells. Humans are unable to detect radiation and, therefore, certain technology has been developed to detect radiation levels for us. This is particularly important for people who regularly work with radiation. One type of technology worn by employees exposed to levels of radiation is the radiation film badge. These badges contain photographic film which turns darker in colour when it absorbs radiation. The more radiation, the darker the film will turn. Workers wear the badges during working hours and check them regularly to assess the level of radiation they have been exposed to, therefore cutting down the risk of exposure to levels of radiation that could damage their health.

The world's worst nuclear accident was that in Chernobyl, in 1986, when one of the four nuclear reactors at the Chernobyl power station exploded, releasing at least 100 times more radiation than the atomic bombs dropped during the Second World War in Nagasaki and Hiroshima. After the accident, the town was evacuated and left abandoned by its people, leaving it looking like a ghost town. A 30 km exclusion zone was set up around the power station, and to this day entry into it is rigidly controlled by checkpoints, due to the existing radiation level. The levels of radiation were so high after the explosion that they could even be detected as far away as Britain, using technology similar to that found in radiation badges. Simple technology such as this provides a means of monitoring safe levels of radiation, critical to the people working and living near radioactive power stations.

The earliest picture of you

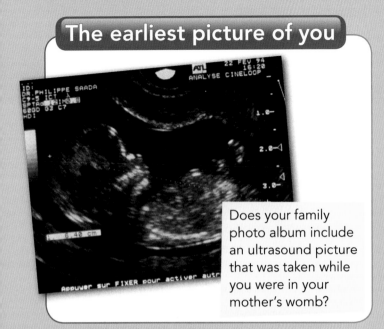

Does your family photo album include an ultrasound picture that was taken while you were in your mother's womb?

Sounds and ultrasounds

All sounds are made from vibrations. Sound travels through air and is detected by our ears. The musical notes that we can hear depends on their frequency and the unit of frequency is the Hertz (Hz). The lowest frequency we can hear is about twenty Hz. The upper range of hearing for humans is about 20 000 Hz (20 kHz). Ultrasounds are beyond this limit and cannot be heard by humans.

The range of hearing reduces during your childhood. Most adults have an upper range of hearing of less than 15 kHz. 'Ultrasonic' ringtones are available and your teachers might not be able to hear these!

Echo, Echo, Echo, Echo, Echo

Have you ever been in a cave or an empty room and heard your voice bounce back to you? Echoes can be good fun but they're also extremely useful.

Bats and whales give out ultrasounds and use the echo to navigate and to detect their prey.

Medical uses of ultrasound

Images can be created from reflected ultrasounds, like the earliest picture of you.

There are several advantages of using ultrasound to look inside the body, especially when monitoring an unborn baby. Ultrasound is safe, it is inexpensive and the machines are portable.

Diagnostic uses of ultrasound

Modern ultrasound images of unborn babies allow doctors and midwives to:

- predict accurately when a baby will be born

- identify if it will be a boy or a girl

- make sure that there are no problems

- find out if twins or more babies are in the womb.

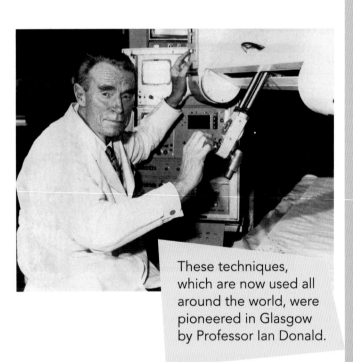

These techniques, which are now used all around the world, were pioneered in Glasgow by Professor Ian Donald.

Therapeutic uses of ultrasound

Ultrasound is now used in a variety of ways and can be focused to clean teeth, break kidney and gall stones, treat cancer and provide a cold water vapour for use in the treatment of asthma.

Commercial uses of health technology

Other technologies, which have become commercially and widely available, include home pregnancy tests, cholesterol monitoring kits and breathalysers to test alcohol levels in the blood.

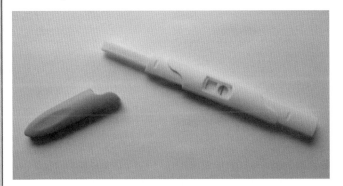

Some companies and sporting organisations routinely carry out blood tests to look for the presence of illegal drugs or steroids in the blood, saliva or hair samples of their employees or sportsmen and women.

Insurance companies can also make use of **nicotine** testing kits, to test the honesty of their clients who claim to be non-smokers. This test searches for the presence of a by-product of nicotine, **cotinine**, and can detect it in the urine up to 72 hours after inhalation of cigarette smoke, thus proving if a person is a smoker or non-smoker.

Technology has helped save lives and improves the quality of lives of millions of people. As a diagnostic tool it can allow the early detection of medical conditions and help put into place preventative measures and effective treatments. Technology has also helped us take responsibility for our own health, as we have developed a fuller understanding at the biological level. This is very important if we are to stay fit and healthy for longer.

The rate of change

Research in science, technology and engineering is increasing all around the world. Much of this is carried out to improve health and quality of life. In hospitals, research has led to the manufacture of an array of amazing cutting-edge and life-saving technologies that allow complicated operations to take place. Organ transplants, open brain surgery and the attachment of artificial limbs are examples of the incredible operations that have become commonplace, thanks to these advances. The use of ventilators to oxygenate blood and vital statistics machines to monitor blood pressure, heart rate and oxygen concentration of the blood, are critical in helping surgeons monitor the health of their patients and help keep them alive. Specialised lasers have been developed to help cut out growths and cancers. Surgeons can use stitches which dissolve without having to be removed. Artificial limbs can be controlled by the person's brain activity. These are all examples of technology that could never have been dreamed of in the distant past.

What can we expect in the future?

Giving blood

Many life-saving operations are only possible because people are willing to donate blood regularly. Despite this, there is currently a general shortage of blood.

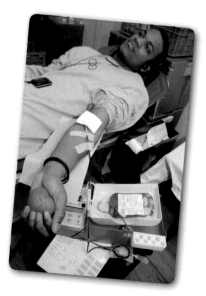

- Why do you think there is a shortage?
- What do you think about donating blood?
- What is your opinion about people who do not donate blood?
- Do you know anyone who has had a blood transfusion?
- What advice would you give people to encourage them to give blood?

Organ donation

What about organ donation? The government are currently debating an opt-out policy for organ donation, because so few people are carrying donor cards.

- What do you think about this?
- Would you donate your organs?
- Is there any reason that you would not or could not donate your organs?

Technological advancement of the century

What do you think has been the most exciting medical technological breakthrough of the twenty-first century? Explain.

GLOSSARY

BP (Abbreviation) blood pressure

Cotinine a harmful chemical found in cigarette smoke

Defibrillator a machine that provides an electric shock to restore the normal heart beat

Diagnosis process of identifying a disease from its signs and symptoms

Electrocardiogram (ECG) diagnoses electrical activity of the heart

Endoscope optical instrument for making a medical examination inside the body

Frequency the number of vibrations in a given time period

Nicotine a harmful chemical found in cigarette smoke

Obesity a medical condition where a person is excessively overweight

Peak flow a measure of how well the lungs are working and can indicate the presence of asthma

Sphygmomanometer instrument for measuring blood pressure

Stethoscope instrument for listening to the heart and lung sounds

Symptoms observed indication of disease

UNESCO (Abbreviation) United Nations Educational, Scientific and Cultural Organization

WHO (Abbreviation) World Health Organization

BIOLOGICAL SYSTEMS
Body Systems and Cells

9

The microscope: Opening an alternative world

Level 2   What came before?

 SCN 2-13a

I have contributed to investigations into the role of micro-organisms in producing and breaking down some materials.

Level 3   What is this chapter about?

 SCN 3-13a

Using a microscope, I have developed my understanding of the structure and variety of cells and their functions.

The microscope: Opening an alternative world

Looking more closely

Scientists use several different types of optical instruments to help them look more closely at objects. Some instruments are used to look at small things more closely, such as hand lenses and microscopes, and others are used to look at objects that are far away, such as binoculars and telescopes.

The Hubble Space Telescope orbits the Earth. This photo was taken by astronauts on board the Space Shuttle Columbia. The telescope has a 10-foot aperture door, which opens to let in light and closes to block out space debris. The solar panels on the telescope provide power, while the foil-like thermal blankets protect Hubble from the extreme temperatures of space.

Using a microscope

We can use a microscope to view cells. This microscope uses lenses to focus light. The objective lens is near to the object that is being observed and the eyepiece lens is at the viewer's eye. The glass slide is supported on the stage of the microscope.

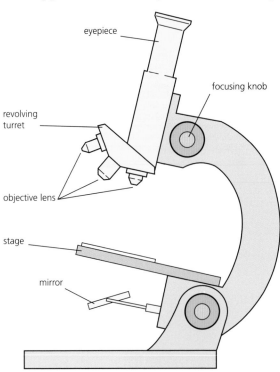

Preparing slides

We need to prepare living things on glass slides in order to see them with a light microscope. Since light has to pass through the object being examined it must be thin. The glass slide used to hold the material must be clean to allow the light to pass through.

1 Place a glass slide on a flat surface.

2 Place a drop of water on the slide from a pipette.

3 Add a specimen to the water on the slide.

4 Hold a cover slip by its sides and lay its bottom edge on the slide.

5 Trap the water between the slide and the cover slip. Gently lower the cover slip with a mounted needle to prevent air bubbles getting trapped.

Here are a set of instructions for using a microscope.

1 Place the slide that you want to look at on the microscope stage.

2 Make sure that the angle of the mirror lets plenty of light up to the slide. (Your microscope may have its own light – make sure it is switched on.)

3 To begin with use the lens with the lowest magnification.

4 With your eye against the eyepiece carefully turn the focus knob until you can see the slide clearly.

5 If you cannot see the material on the slide clearly, you may have to use the more powerful lens.

Most microscopes have up to three different objective lenses, which allow a low, medium and high level of magnification. The focus control is used to achieve a clear image of the material.

Investigating cells with a microscope can be difficult; particularly animal cells as they tend to be smaller than plant cells. Their flexible outer layer – the cell membrane – means the cell shape can be altered when the microscope slide is being prepared.

It is often confusing to look at cells with a microscope and scientists use stains to improve the appearance of the cells. The stain is a dye that helps to highlight one or more parts of the cell.

Single-celled organisms

The microscope allows us to see structures that are too small to be seen by the human eye. If a drop of pond water is examined under the microscope, tiny creatures can be seen swimming about. They have strange appearances and even stranger names – **Paramecium** or **Amoeba** (pronounced Para-meesy-um and A-me-ba).

These tiny living organisms have only one compartment or cell in which all the living processes occur. All living things are made of cells – they are the basic unit of living things. (But more about what cells are later.)

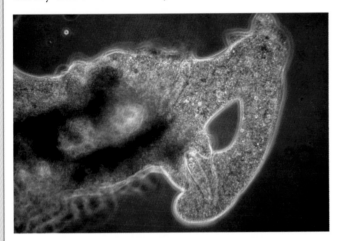

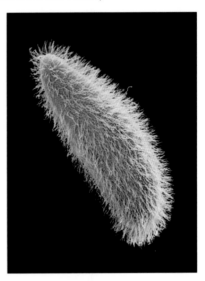

Active Learning ▶

Activity

Find out about other single-celled organisms.

Multi-cellular organisms

Some of the other tiny organisms living in the pond, such as **rotifers** and **cyclops**, are multi-cellular – they have more than one cell.

Large living things are made of many cells. Human beings are made from **trillions** of cells. If human tissue is examined under the microscope then we can see that there are many different types of cells in a multi-cellular organism. Can you suggest a reason why?

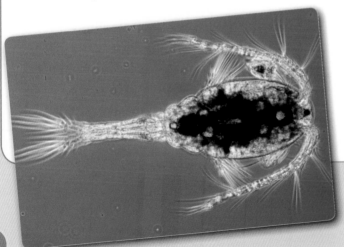

Big numbers: Find out how many thousands make a million and how many million make a trillion.

⇨

Multi-cellular organisms

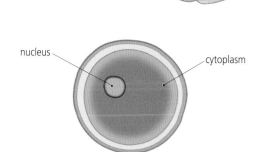

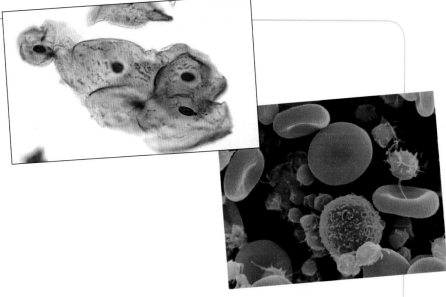

Look at the photographs of the cells shown. Each of these cells has a different job to do. Each cell has special features to help it carry out its function. For example, the egg cell has a large food store to help it grow if it is fertilised.

What is a cell?

All living organisms are made from units called **cells**. Huge numbers of different types of cells exist and they each have different appearances. Although different types of cell look different from each other, they do have many things in common. They have a thin covering around them called a **cell membrane**. They have a watery gel inside the cell, called **cytoplasm** (pronounced sigh-toe-plas-m) and they have a round dense area inside the cell called a **nucleus**.

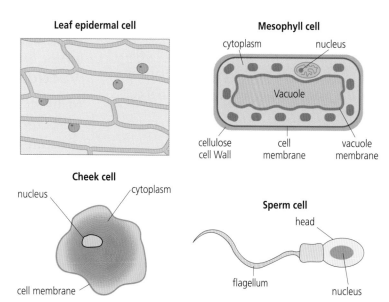

Leaf epidermal cell

Mesophyll cell

cytoplasm — nucleus

Vacuole

cellulose cell Wall — cell membrane — vacuole membrane

Cheek cell

nucleus — cytoplasm

cell membrane

Sperm cell

head

flagellum

nucleus

The cell membrane is the boundary of the cell but it also controls the movement of chemicals in and out of the cell. The jelly-like cytoplasm is filled with dissolved raw materials and **enzymes**. This is the site of most of the cell's chemical reactions e.g. those that make heat and those that manufacture and store new materials. The nucleus contains **genetic** information contained in structures called **chromosomes**. This information controls everything that the cell is able to do e.g. leaf cells carry out photosynthesis, nerve cells pass on electrical messages. The nucleus is able to divide and make new cells so that living things are able to grow and to repair damaged parts of the organism.

Recognising plant cells

Look at the plant cell below.

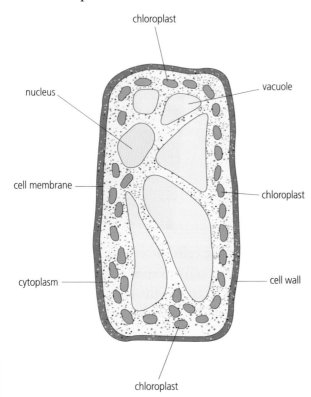

The cell membrane, nucleus and cytoplasm are common to all cells. Look again at the plant cells on page 97. Can you see some structures that are present in the plant cell but not in the animal cells?

Cell walls

All plant cells have an outer wall which surrounds the cell membrane. This makes plant cells more rigid and regular in shape than animal cells. Cell walls are made of a substance called **cellulose**.

Cellulose looks like a mat of fibres when it is magnified several thousand times. This helps its properties of allowing materials, e.g. water, to pass in and out of the cell as well as making it flexible.

Chloroplasts

From studying cells under the microscope we can see that cells have smaller compartments within them such as a nucleus and chloroplasts. The smaller structures are called cell **organelles**.

The cells in leaves and other green parts of plants have structures in their cytoplasm called chloroplasts. Animal cells never have chloroplasts.

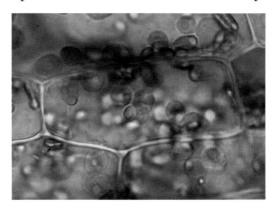

Photosynthesis takes place inside the chloroplasts. Each chloroplast is able to trap light energy and use it to make sugars and oxygen.

Vacuoles

Many plant cells have an area inside the cytoplasm where the plant cell stores water and salts. This structure is called a **vacuole**. The vacuole has its own membrane around it.

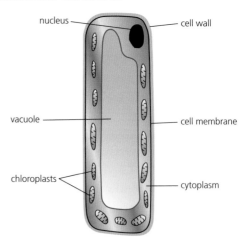

Although the vacuole looks like it is filled with nothing much but water, it is a very important part of the plant cell because it:

- Helps support the leaves and other soft tissues (think about what a plant looks like when it wilts).

- Stores waste and harmful substances.

- Regulates the cell's pH.

The commercial uses of cellulose

Cellulose is an amazing material. The **nanofibres** allow it to be flexible. Living plants are able to move freely in wind and water currents. Their roots are able to grow and force their way into the narrowest spaces that exist in the soil. The cellulose cell wall in each plant allows the passage of water into and out of the cell, helping the soft part of the plant to remain upright. In many plants the cellulose is chemically changed into a harder, less flexible material called **lignin**. All woody materials contain large proportions of lignin.

Mankind uses and adapts cellulose as a raw material in an enormous number of ways because it is an inexpensive, naturally occurring raw material.

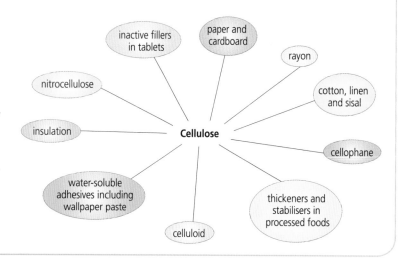

The same but different?

Multi-cellular organisms include a variety of different cell types. Cells in your body are specialised to carry out different jobs. Muscle cells that make you move appear quite different under the microscope compared with liver cells.

Each cell is designed to make it efficient at carrying out a particular function. This is the same for all multi-cellular organisms. However, there are some functions that all cells have in common.

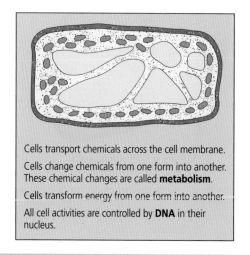

MUSCLE CELLS

C ontract for movement
E xcellent I'd say
L ocomotion is not possible in
L iver cells you
S ee

Cells transport chemicals across the cell membrane.

Cells change chemicals from one form into another. These chemical changes are called **metabolism**.

Cells transform energy from one form into another.

All cell activities are controlled by **DNA** in their nucleus.

Cell specialisation

In multi-cellular organisms cells have become specialised to allow them to carry out a particular function. For example, in mammals the only type of cell that can produce movement is a muscle cell.

Thick Filament

Thin Filament

Muscle cells have a nucleus, cytoplasm and a cell membrane but they also have special fibres that allow them to contract (become smaller). This is how they bring about movement. When you raise your arm the muscle cells contract and this is what causes the arm to lift up.

Food is moved through your digestive system by muscles. Your heart contains a powerful muscle.

Cell organisation - tissues

A living organism is highly organised. Cells of the same type work together in different parts of the body to perform the same thing. These collections of similar cells are called **tissues**. Examples of tissues in your body include: muscle, skin, liver and bone tissue. Specialised tissues often work with other ones. For example muscle tissue and nervous tissue work together in the heart to control the pump for propelling blood around the body.

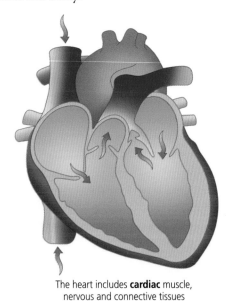

The heart includes **cardiac** muscle, nervous and connective tissues

Cell organisation – organs

Structures that have several tissues working together are called organs. There are many organs in your body – here are some of them:

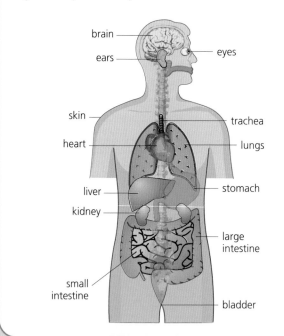

brain
ears
eyes
skin
heart
trachea
lungs
liver
stomach
kidney
large intestine
small intestine
bladder

Cell organisation – organ systems

Just as tissues work together to form organs; organs work together to form the **systems** of your body e.g. the trachea and the lungs are part of the respiratory system; the sensory system includes the eyes, ears, skin and brain; the central nervous system includes the brain and the spinal cord.

A system has organs and tissues working together to perform particular functions such as digestion and absorption of food. The cells, tissues, organs and systems combine to make the whole organism.

QUESTIONS

1   📖 The first person to identify cells was an English scientist called Robert Hooke. Find out more about Robert Hooke.

2   Make a flow chart to show the stages involved in looking at a prepared slide with a microscope.

3   Organise the information about the function of the different parts of the cell into a table.

4   Find out about stem cells. What is different about them compared to other types of cell?

5   📖 Research **one** kind of cell from **one** type of tissue in your body. Make a poster labelled with the cell type, their parts and their functions.

Examples:

a) epithelial tissue

b) connective tissue

c) muscle tissue

d) the nervous tissue.

6   Find out the names of three organs in the human body and the systems that they are part of.

Cell biology and research science

The scientific study of cells has helped our understanding of the structure of the cell and how it works. This information has led to a greater understanding of many diseases such as cancer, heart disease and Alzheimer's disease. In turn this has led to new treatments for many diseases.

Here are photographs of some onion cells and some cheek cells that were taken with a digital camera that was attached to a microscope.

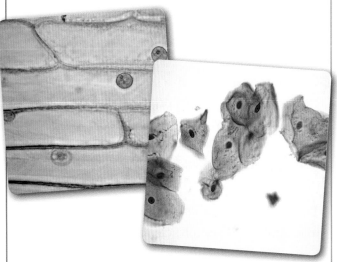

Cells are truly remarkable things but a lot of their parts cannot be seen with a light microscope; how they behave and many of their properties can only be shown by carrying out experiments. Research scientists are keen to copy the clever things that cells can do.

Chloroplasts are efficient at capturing light and transforming it into chemical energy. Research scientists are searching for materials that copy or even improve this process.

The **cellulose cell wall** surrounds plant cells. It provides food for **herbivores**. Renewable biofuels are created by fermenting cellulose to produce ethanol. Research scientists are trying to improve biofuel production in order to reduce the use of fossil fuels.

⇨

Cell biology and research science

Movement takes place inside cells. Many cells are also able to move. This is brought about by proteins which transform chemicals to kinetic energy. Research scientists are trying to find out more about this movement in order to create nano-machines, switches and power sources.

Cell membranes are able to sense tiny quantities of chemical substances. They can then allow them to enter the cell or keep them out. They can even trap harmful and unwanted materials. Research scientists are investigating ways of using this to deliver drugs to cancerous cells with **nano-particles** and are excited at the prospect of using cells to detect security threats such as explosives or drugs.

Cell membranes are also sensitive to minute electrical changes. This property makes the whole nervous system work. Research scientists are interested in helping damaged nerves and brain tissue to heal and restore their former functions.

The **cytoplasm** is able to convert one substance into another. Research scientists often use cells to manufacture medicines and other materials.

The **nucleus** is wrapped up in a membrane and contains the chromosomes which are made from DNA and proteins. DNA contains the genetic instructions for every living thing. It is able to copy itself when new cells are made. Research scientists are exploring materials that copy and repair themselves.

The scale of life

 The metre (m) is the unit in which length is measured. It can be divided into one thousandths and this unit is called a millimetre (mm).

Although one millimetre is the smallest unit in a ruler it is still much bigger than a single cell.

Cell size is measured in microns or micrometres. A micron is one thousandth of a millimetre.

The symbol for a micron is µ. (This Greek letter is pronounced 'Mew'.)

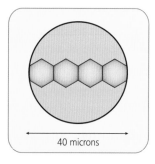

40 microns

Calculate

The cell shown above is 40µ in length. How many of these cells could be placed side by side in a line one millimetre in length?

Representations of cells, drawings or photographs are always much bigger than the actual cell. To indicate this, the diagram may be labelled '×100', indicating that the image has been multiplied 100 times.

Map makers have the opposite problem when drawing maps. Maps have to be much smaller than the real thing but, like the best drawings of cells, they must be drawn to scale.

It's all in the detail – magnifying things even more

The type of microscope used in school laboratories is a light microscope. Microscopes allow us to look at things more closely. Some scientists use microscopes to look at living materials and cells, and others use them to look at crystals, at electronic components and microchips. They even use them to look at thin slices of rocks. Light is directed by a mirror or from a lamp through a thin piece of tissue, for example some bone tissue. The light then travels through curved pieces of glass called lenses. It is the effect of the lenses on the light rays that cause the specimen to appear larger. This effect is called magnification.

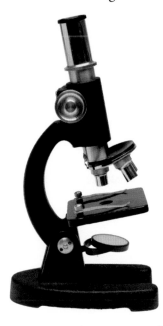

In the light microscope there are two lenses. One is called the **objective** lens and is placed close to the specimen. The other is called the **eyepiece** lens and it is the one we look through. The magnification is calculated by multiplying the individual magnifying power of each of the lenses. If the objective lens has a magnification of ×10 and the eyepiece lens has a magnification of ×10 then the magnification will be ×100 (10 multiplied by 10).

Eyepiece lens magnification × objective lens magnification = total magnification.

There are limits to how much magnification a light microscope can achieve. The very best ones can magnify up to ×1500 but scientists want to look closer still – maybe even as many as a million times magnification! They achieve these levels of magnification with another type of microscope, called the **electron microscope**.

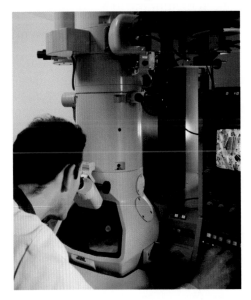

The electron microscope uses a beam of electrons rather than light. Studying cells with this microscope has revealed incredible detail of the structure inside the cell. The electron microscope allows scientist to look even more closely at cells and see even more details and structures that are not visible using a light microscope.

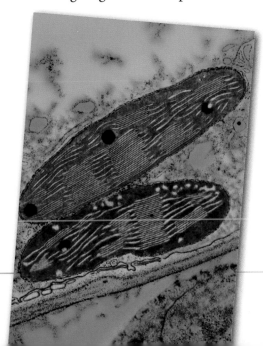

GLOSSARY

Amoeba pond animal made of one cell only

Cell membrane layer that surrounds every cell

Cell wall made of cellulose and surrounds plant cells' membranes

Cellulose grows as fibres which surround the cell membrane to form the cell wall

Chloroplast organelle where photosynthesis takes place

Cyclops multi-cellular pond animal

Cytoplasm fluid that fills cells

Enzyme protein that controls chemical reactions inside cells

Genetic (Adjective) relating to genetics – something that can be inherited

Lignin tough woody fibres in plant material

Nanofibre fibres with tiny diameters (less than 100 nm)

Nanoparticle tiny particle (size between 100 and 2500 nm)

Nucleus organelle surrounded by double membrane which directs all of the cell activities

Organ body structure that is made up of several tissues

Organelle a specialised part of a cell

Paramecium pond animal made of one cell only

Rotifer multi-cellular pond animal

Stem cell cell that is capable of reproducing and specialising in a number of different ways

Tissue identical cells that carry out similar functions

Vacuole store of water and nutrients inside plant cells

BIOLOGICAL SYSTEMS
Body Systems and Cells

10
Microbes and you

Level 2 — What came before?

 SCN 2-13a

I have contributed to investigations into the role of micro-organisms in producing and breaking down some materials.

Level 3 — What is this chapter about?

 SCN 3-13b

I have contributed to investigations into the different types of micro-organisms and can explain how their growth can be controlled.

Microbes and you

Have you ever thought of yourself as a living zoo?

Think about this.....

Growing on your skin, in your mouth, throughout your intestines and everywhere around you there are huge numbers of microbes, living organisms too small to be seen without the use of a powerful microscope.

As many as 300 kinds of bacteria live in your mouth, make **plaque** and cause dental decay.

Do you know that every spoonful of bio-yoghurt contains tens of thousands of living lactic acid bacteria?

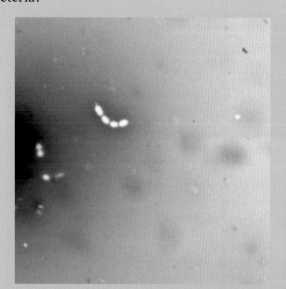

The terms 'microbes' or 'micro-organisms' are used to describe microscopic living things e.g. bacteria, viruses, fungi, algae and protozoa.

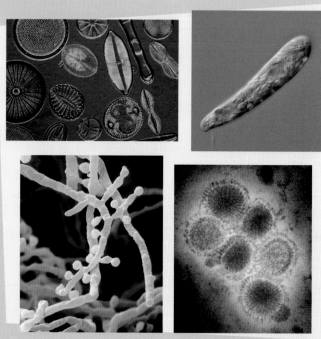

The scientific study of microbes is termed 'microbiology' and the individuals who investigate them are called 'microbiologists'.

Microbes are found everywhere on planet Earth. From the summits of the highest mountains to the trenches of the deepest oceans and from the hottest habitats to the coldest places on earth, you will find microbes adapted to survive there.

Micro-organisms affect every aspect of our lives. They help and hinder us, cause disease and help to treat disease. They are a source of food but they also cause food to spoil. Many microbes benefit humankind, and some microbes provide huge challenges.

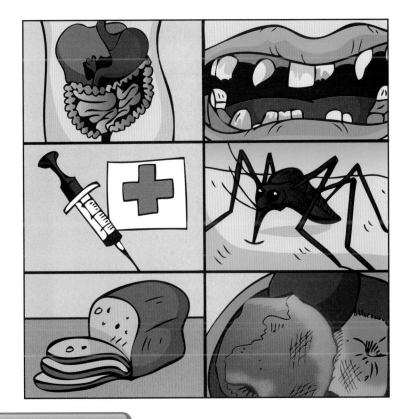

Beneficial microbes – the good guys

Yeast industries

Brewing and baking are major industries which involve yeast, a group of single-celled fungi. These processes have been undertaken for many centuries. They both depend on the yeast turning sugar into carbon dioxide, alcohol and heat. The carbon dioxide makes bread rise and makes beer fizz. The alcohol evaporates from the bread during baking; and most of the gas in brewing goes into the atmosphere.

Sugar → Carbon dioxide + Alcohol + Heat

Antibiotics

Biotechnology companies are constantly developing enterprising methods of making use of microbes to benefit humankind and for commercial success. Fungi produce **antibiotics** in an effort to reduce the competition from bacteria. Humans use these antibiotics to fight disease caused by bacteria.

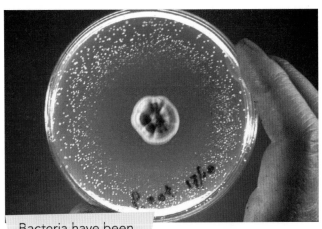

Bacteria have been killed by the mould.

Beneficial microbes – the good guys

Active Learning ▶

Activity

📖 Research one of the following with a partner, group or by yourself. Present your findings in a poster or write a report.

- The discovery of Penicillin by Alexander Fleming.
- The role of Florey and Chain in the development of penicillin.
- The commercial production of penicillin.
- The wide range of antibiotics.
- Antibiotic resistance.
- MRSA.
- Diseases effectively treated by antibiotics.
- Use of antibiotics with domestic cattle.
- Use of antibiotics with farmed salmon.

Natural recycling

Microbes play an essential role in the cycles of life; they recycle the nutrients of the dead and the waste of living things. All waste produced by organisms will become food for micro-organisms, which will break down the waste and recycle the minerals and nutrients present in the waste. Eventually when an organism dies it will be recycled by the action of micro-organisms and establish new food chains.

The Nitrogen Cycle

Only certain groups of bacteria can capture nitrogen from our atmosphere and convert it into nitrates.

The nodules in these roots are packed with nitrogen-fixing bacteria.

Nitrates are needed by plants to manufacture protein which in turn provides the raw materials for proteins in all food chains. Nitrogen returns to the atmosphere when living things decompose.

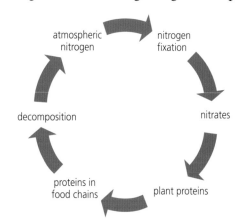

By studying the structure and function of the genes of microbes, scientists aim to gain a better understanding of how they work. This allows the development of better antimicrobial medicines and allows other microbes to work efficiently in a wide range of biotechnology industries e.g. the manufacture of human growth hormone and human insulin within a bacterial cell.

Viruses are being used to carry genes (bits of DNA which code for specific proteins to be manufactured) into the nucleus of other organisms to modify and improve their functions.

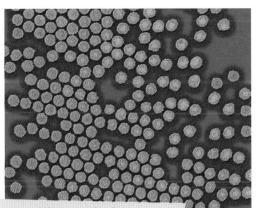

You are protected from polio by vaccination. Weak or inactivated viruses are used in polio vaccine production.

Microbes assist with cleaning up the environment. Certain bacteria and protozoa break down sewage into water and carbon dioxide. The outflow from sewage works can then be safely released into rivers.

The microscopic algae in the oceans are called **phytoplankton**.

Phytoplankton is the major producer in oceanic food chains and is reported to manufacture 70% of the oxygen in every breath that we take.

These microbes trap carbon dioxide and convert its atoms into the carbohydrate structure of life. Without microbes, all life on Earth would cease to exist.

Disease-causing microbes – the bad guys

Bacterial diseases

Bacteria cause many illnesses including plague, tuberculosis, typhoid, cholera, forms of pneumonia and meningitis, food poisoning and certain sexually transmitted diseases.

Pale yellow colonies of tuberculosis bacteria growing on a green culture medium.

Black Death

In the thirteenth and fourteenth centuries plague ravaged Europe. The Bubonic Plague, commonly known as the Black Death, killed an estimated 40 million people. This meant that one person died out of every three living at that time.

The Plague was caused by a rod-shaped bacterium *Yersinia pestis* which was carried by rats and passed to humans in flea bites. If the bacteria spread from the blood to the lungs it developed into the pneumonic form of plague, which spread easily in the atmosphere when people coughed and sneezed. No treatment was available and about half the infected people died from the Plague as the bacteria grew and multiplied in their bloodstream.

We can treat diseases with antibiotics now but the rapid evolution of resistance to antibiotics developed by certain bacteria means that the pharmaceutical industry has to constantly develop new antibiotics or modify the chemical structure of antibiotics already in use.

Viral diseases

Viruses cause illnesses such as the common cold, measles, chickenpox, influenza, AIDS and rabies.

Fungal diseases

Fungi cause infections such as athlete's foot, thrush and dandruff.

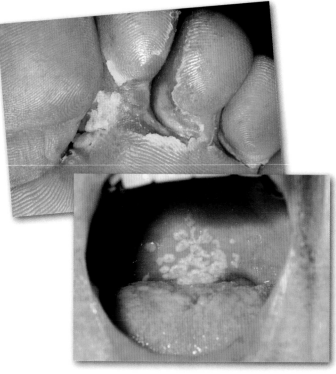

Protozoan diseases

Protozoan diseases include malaria and sleeping sickness. These are two of the world's most serious fatal diseases.

Fungal infections often cause further problems when the body's immune system has been affected by stress, other microbes (e.g. HIV) or when drugs have been given to reduce the chances of donated organs being rejected.

QUESTIONS

1 Five groups of micro-organisms have been described in this chapter. Make a table to summarise key points about each of these groups.

2 Describe the importance of micro-organisms in nature. Make reference to recycling and how they fit into food chains.

3 Research more about:

   a) recent pandemics

   b) food poisoning

   c) fermentation and industry.

Controlling the growth of microbes

Biomedical scientists, who often work in hospital laboratories, investigate samples taken from patients to enable them to grow and identify microbes which cause disease. Disease-causing micro-organisms are called **pathogens**. The scientists' aim is to identify suitable treatments and to prevent the spread of infection in operating theatres, hospital wards and the wider community.

Disease prevention is absolutely crucial to humankind. During the late nineteenth century much was learned about how diseases were spread. Sources of public water supplies were improved to provide clean, safe drinking water.

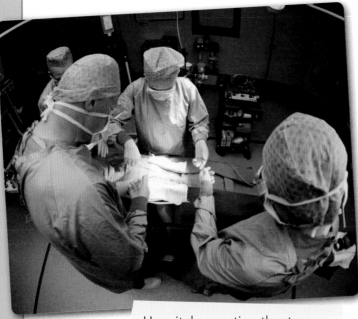

Hospital operating theatres must be kept very clean to prevent infection spreading. Instruments are always sterile.

Public water supplies are constantly monitored to ensure that they are safe. Improved domestic sanitation and effective treatment of sewage resulted in diseases such as typhoid and cholera becoming uncommon in most of Western Europe.

Sadly, many parts of Africa and Asia are still gravely affected by the bacteria which cause these infections. The spread of infectious diseases is studied and monitored by the World Health Organisation.

The outbreak of the influenza H1N1 (Swine flu) virus demonstrated that the threat of epidemics and **pandemics** remains very real.

The control of microbial contamination is very important in the food industry. Safe food storage relies on preventing spoilage by the growth of microbes. Spoiled food looks and smells bad but, much more seriously, the spoiled foods may contain microbes, which are **pathogens** (these cause human disease). Contamination of food, especially frozen food, with *Salmonella, Listeria* and *Campylobacter* bacteria result in serious illnesses which sometimes make the news headlines.

Controlling the growth of microbes

Many methods of controlling microbial growth in food have been developed to prevent the spread of infection. Some of these approaches have been used since ancient times, e.g. salting, drying and pickling.

Several spices inhibit bacterial growth. Cloves and cinnamon have been used for centuries to preserve food. Other food additives e.g. potassium nitrite are used to preserve meat, such as bacon.

Fish were smoked in pits over open fires to preserve them for longer periods of time. The Arbroath Smokie is haddock caught in the North Sea that has been smoked over oak and beechwood smoke in the town of Arbroath. Smoke has some antibacterial properties and also adds flavour to the fish.

Aseptic beginnings

A walk through old graveyards reading the inscriptions reveals that many mothers and their children died during or soon after childbirth. Many of these deaths were caused by infection from micro-organisms. At Glasgow Royal Infirmary in 1867, Joseph Lister developed aseptic surgical techniques when he started to use a spray of carbolic acid during hospital operations. The carbolic acid acted as a **germicide** and reduced the number of patients dying from wound infections after surgery by up to 45%. Since then the control of microbial growth has saved many lives and has developed into a hugely profitable industry.

The term **sepsis** comes from a Greek word meaning to decay. Decay of organic matter results from contamination by bacteria and fungi. The opposite of sepsis is **asepsis**. Aseptic techniques were developed by Lister and are used to prevent contamination of instruments, wounds and individuals during surgical operations. These techniques are also used in the food and biotechnology industries to prevent contamination and spoilage.

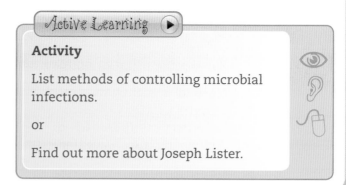

Active Learning ▶

Activity

List methods of controlling microbial infections.

or

Find out more about Joseph Lister.

The effect of high temperatures on microbial growth

Micro-organisms are destroyed by the process called sterilisation. The most common sterilising agent is heat. Heating destroys (**denatures**) the enzymes which allow the microbes to function and also destroys other proteins which give the microbe its structure. The ability to cope with heat varies between species. Moist heat (e.g. steam) is known to destroy microbes much more efficiently than dry heat. Some microbes can withstand harsh environmental conditions by producing inactive, tough capsules called spores. Spores are able to **disperse** bacteria in air and water.

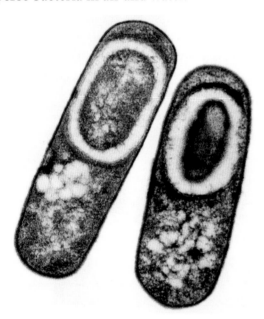

Spores can even survive in boiling water at 100 °C. The spores are, however, destroyed in an autoclave,

which is really a big pressure cooker, and this raises the temperature in the chamber to more than 121 °C.

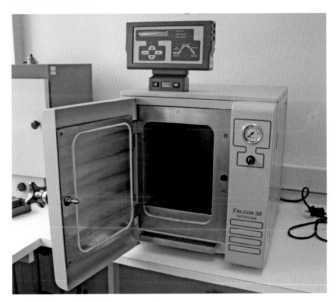

Canned foods are heat-treated to destroy bacterial spores – *Clostridium botulinum* in particular. This bacterium produces botox **toxin** which causes muscle paralysis and is often fatal to infected people.

Active Learning ▶

Activity

Research how an autoclave works.

or

Research the use of botox techniques.

Disinfectants

Disinfectants are used to reduce the number of disease-causing microbes on non-living things. Antiseptics are used on living tissue that would be destroyed by disinfectants. Alcohol wipes are used to remove most bacteria from a surface or an area of skin.

Unfortunately there is not one disinfectant that is suitable for all situations. Each of the methods has advantages and disadvantages.

Hand washing

Warm soapy water used regularly to wash hands will remove disease-causing microbes and limit the spread of infection.

Activity

Design your own poster to encourage hand washing.

Now wash your hands

Active chemicals

Certain chemicals are said to be **Bacteriostatic**. These chemicals stop or slow down the growth of bacteria but the bacteria are not killed. **Germicides** kill some micro-organisms. **Bactericides** kill bacteria but not most spores. A **viricide** is used to stop the action of viruses. Fungi are killed by **fungicides**. Bacterial spores are destroyed by **sporicides**.

Toiletries and cosmetics have preservatives added to them to ensure that contamination by microbes is not a problem. Quorn, a foodstuff manufactured from fungi, is grown under sterile conditions.

The starter kits used to grow mushrooms commercially are also grown under sterile conditions.

Pasteurisation

Some materials that need to be sterilised are damaged by the pressure, heat and moisture used in this steam sterilisation process.

The process of **pasteurisation** was developed by the great nineteenth-century French scientist Louis Pasteur to prevent spoilage of liquids. Pasteurisation is used to limit contamination of milk, wine, beer and fruit juices by heating the liquid to 65 °C for 30 minutes.

Pasteurised milk is now heated to 72 °C for 15 seconds. UHT milk (Ultra High Temperature pasteurisation) involves the milk being heated at 140 °C for 3 seconds and then cooled rapidly. This allows the milk to be stored in a sealed container at room temperature for several months.

Flaming

Microbes and their spores cannot survive the high temperatures generated by flames in an **incinerator**. Microbiologists use inoculating loops and needles to transfer bacteria between cultures. They sterilise equipment directly in a flame until the metal develops a red glow.

Incineration sterilises contaminated wound dressings, surgical swabs and other materials by burning all disposable items.

Low temperatures

The low temperatures found in fridges (4 °C) have bacteriostatic effects on most microbes and it greatly reduces their ability to multiply or to produce toxins which lead to spoilage of food. Slow freezing causes ice crystals to form in cells and this may kill many micro-organisms.

Drying out (desiccation)

Removing all the water from microbes leads to them drying out. This process stops the microbes growing and reproducing. Some may remain alive for many years and will only start growing and dividing again when water becomes available in their environment. Viruses are generally resistant to drying out. The germs which cause tuberculosis survive in a dry state for months.

Sugars and salts

High concentrations of salts and sugars remove the water from microbes by the process of **osmosis** and ensure that fish stored in salt (e.g. shrimps in brine) and pots of jam remain uncontaminated by microbes for lengthy periods. The microbes may not die, they simply may stop growing and reproducing.

Yeasts and moulds may be found growing on old pots of jam as they are more able to cope with less water in their environments.

Radiation

Microbes are destroyed by radiation. X-rays and gamma rays are used to sterilise certain medicines and other medical items e.g. plastic petri dishes. Radiation destroys DNA and prevents cells reproducing.

UV light is used to reduce microbial contamination in operating theatres, butcher's shops and kitchens.

People must also be protected from harmful UV radiation.

Radiation has been used to sterilise these petri dishes. People must be protected from harmful radiation while using this technique.

Chemicals used in the control of growth of microbes

Many different chemicals are used to control microbial growth.

Lister first used carbolic acid as a disinfectant. This is rarely used now as it has a strong smell and irritates human skin.

Iodine added to alcohol was known as 'tincture of iodine' and this was one of the first antiseptics. It denatures proteins, stains skin and anything else it gets on to and is an irritant.

Chlorine is added to drinking water and in higher volumes to swimming pools. It forms a disinfectant acid when mixed with water. Bleach also acts to inhibit microbial growth.

Alcohols denature proteins and kill bacteria and fungi. Surgical spirit contains alcohol which is effective in preventing infection but is very painful when first applied to an open wound.

Certain metal salts inhibit microbial growth, e.g. silver and copper. Copper sulphate is used sometimes to limit growth of microbes in fish tanks.

Selenium and zinc salts are used to kill fungi and they are found in anti dandruff shampoos.

Active Learning

Investigation

An investigation into the effect of disinfectants and antiseptics on microbial growth.

Aims

To observe, describe and compare the effect of disinfectants and antiseptics on bacteria growing on nutrient agar plates.

Method   **WEAR SAFETY GOGGLES**

A selection of disinfectants e.g. Milton fluid, Domestos, Toilet Duck, bleach, Jeyes Fluid, may be dipped with sterile filter paper or directly added to wells cut in Petri dishes containing nutrient agar. Antiseptic creams may be dissolved in water and added to wells or dipped with sterile filter paper discs cut with cork borers.

Zones of clearing where no bacteria have grown may then be observed and measured.

QUESTIONS

1 Why do disinfectants and antiseptics not always result in sterilisation?

2 Explain the difference between disinfectants and antiseptics.

3 Why are disinfectants not used as mouth or throat gargles to treat microbial infections?

4 Write a paragraph to explain the zones of clearing that appear around the wells filled with antimicrobial chemicals.

Active Learning ▶

Research

📖 Find out 10 facts about one of the following and present them in a poster:

- Joseph Lister
- Louis Pasteur
- the autoclave
- chemical toilets
- Milton fluid
- mouthwash
- anti-dandruff shampoos
- surgical sterilisation.

GLOSSARY

Antibiotic chemical produced by living things that can stop other ones from growing

Asepsis free from micro-organisms

Bactericide an agent that destroys bacteria

Bacteriostatic a chemical that prevents further growth of bacteria

Denature change the natural properties of a substance

Desiccation remove water

Disperse scatter and travel to a new place

Fungicide an agent that destroys fungi

Germicide an agent that destroys germs

Incinerator a container that burns waste and is of a sufficiently high temperature to kill all living things

Microbe a tiny living thing, micro-organism – often refers to the bacteria which cause disease

Microbiology the scientific study of microbes

Micro-organism a living thing that is too small to see without a microscope

Osmosis process in living things that allows water to diffuse in and out of cells

Pandemic a disease epidemic which covers a large area and affects unusually high numbers of the population

Pasteurisation process of killing pathogenic microbes in liquids e.g. milk and wine

Pathogen a disease-causing organism

Phytoplankton microscopic plants that are found in fresh water and in seawater

Radiation energy in the form of rays and waves

Sepsis the presence of pathogens and their poisonous waste in living tissues

Sporicide an agent that destroys spores

Toxin a poisonous chemical released from pathogens

BIOLOGICAL SYSTEMS

Body Systems and Cells

11
Under attack

Level 3   What is this chapter about?

 SCN 3-13c

I have explored how the body defends itself against disease and I can describe how vaccines can provide protection.

Under attack

Micro-organisms that cause disease, **pathogens**, may infect the cells of the body causing illness and, in some cases, death. To prevent this from happening, the body has a number of defence mechanisms that work together and make up the **immune system**.

There are several different **defence mechanisms** that the body uses to protect itself from disease. The first line of defence involves a number of physical barriers and fluids that prevent pathogenic micro-organisms from reaching the body's internal cell environment.

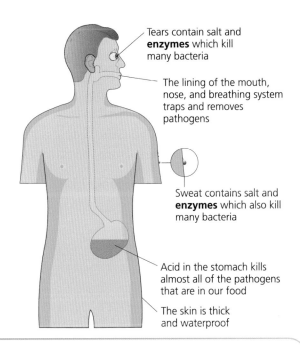

Tears contain salt and **enzymes** which kill many bacteria

The lining of the mouth, nose, and breathing system traps and removes pathogens

Sweat contains salt and **enzymes** which also kill many bacteria

Acid in the stomach kills almost all of the pathogens that are in our food

The skin is thick and waterproof

Skin – the great barrier

The skin is a very effective physical barrier between your external environment and the internal environment of body cells.

The skin is the body's largest organ. It is thicker in some parts of your body than it is on other parts. But what else do you know about your skin?

Active Learning ▶

Activity

Look carefully at your skin.

List 10 things you know about it and then compare your list with a classmate. How many different things do the class know about skin?

Have you ever suffered from sunburn?

Sunburn is sore! It can be really harmful as well.

Mild sunburn can be treated at home by drinking lots of water, using a moisturising cream and cooling the affected area. The outer layer of the skin will peel off but quickly recover.

People who suffer from sunburn have an increased risk of suffering from skin cancer, also called melanoma. We should protect our skin from harmful ultraviolet rays which we cannot feel but which have harmful effects on the skin. The best way to avoid skin damage is to protect your skin the following ways:

Skin – the great barrier

Skin layers

The reason that your skin peels if you have suffered from sunburn is that it is made up of several layers. The outer one is dead and is removed as your skin rubs against your clothes as well as each time you wash your skin. A lot of household dust is made of skin which has fallen away from the skin surface!

Here is what a block of skin looks like:

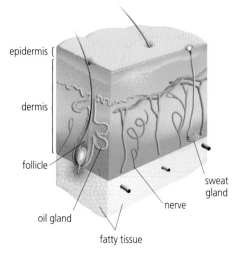

epidermis

dermis

follicle

oil gland

fatty tissue

nerve

sweat gland

Skin protects you from invaders

No micro-organisms can enter the immediate cell surroundings unless there is a cut to the skin. When this happens it is called **infection**. Normally a scab will form over a cut to create a temporary barrier to infection until the skin underneath heals.

However, not all pathogens are likely to enter your body through contact with the skin. For example, micro-organisms may be present in the air we breathe in or on the food we swallow. As a consequence, the body must have other ways of preventing pathogens from reaching body cells and causing disease.

Tears

Tears are the liquid that is released by your tear ducts. Tears bathe your eyes to keep them moist, washing away dust and dirt. They also lubricate the eye and allow it to move smoothly inside the socket.

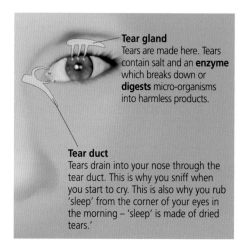

Tear gland
Tears are made here. Tears contain salt and an **enzyme** which breaks down or **digests** micro-organisms into harmless products.

Tear duct
Tears drain into your nose through the tear duct. This is why you sniff when you start to cry. This is also why you rub 'sleep' from the corner of your eyes in the morning – 'sleep' is made of dried tears.'

Mucus and cilia

The air tubes of your breathing system, i.e. the passages of your nose, trachea and bronchi, are lined with a sticky substance called **mucus** (pronounced 'mew-kus'). This material traps dirt and micro-organisms and stops them reaching the lungs. Tiny muscular hairs called **cilia** are also present on the surface of the cells that line these tubes. They sweep the 'dirty' mucus towards the mouth where we cough it out or swallow it into the stomach.

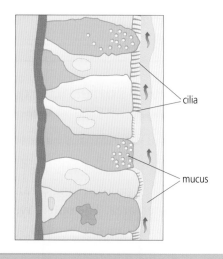

cilia

mucus

Stomach acid

The acid conditions in your stomach make it difficult for micro-organisms to grow, effectively destroying any **pathogens** that might be swallowed in mucus or as part of the food we eat. This prevents pathogenic molecules reaching body cells via the digestive system.

Active Learning ▶

Activity

Use the Internet to find the following information:

1 Find out the name of the enzyme that is present in tears which destroys pathogens.

2 List the names of the tubes in the breathing system which are lined with cilia and mucus.

3 Find out the name of the cells that produce mucus in the breathing system.

4 Find out the name of the acid present in the stomach and its pH value.

5 Research other enzymes that digest or break down molecules in a similar way to the one present in our tears. You can work in a small group to produce a leaflet or poster. Explain how and where they work, which molecules they break down and what is made as a product of each reaction.

Weapons of mass destruction

There are times when micro-organisms manage to penetrate the body's first line of defence and can reach the internal environment of the body. In such situations, the body cells themselves are at risk of being infected. If this happens a second line of defence is needed whereby pathogens are **engulfed** and **destroyed** while in the body fluids, before they make contact with our cells.

Our immune system produces specialised **white blood cells** called **phagocytes** which perform this function.

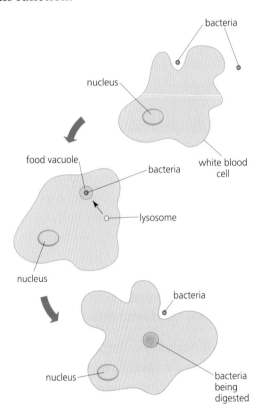

This is called a **macrophage**, which means 'big eater'. It wraps around the pathogen, engulfing it into the cell where enzymes then digest the micro-organism into harmless molecules. The enzymes inside the macrophage are stored in a small structure called a **lysosome** which has its own membrane around it so that the enzymes don't damage any of the cell contents.

Weapons of mass destruction

A non-specific response

Phagocytosis is an example of an **immune response**. This is when your body's immune system reacts to the presence of something that has entered your body. This type of immune response is 'non-specific'. This means that phagocytes will engulf and destroy any materials and micro-organisms that are present in the body and are potentially harmful.

Along with tears, mucus production, cilia and stomach acid, the ability to carry out phagocytosis is present from birth. This means we are born with some (**innate**) **immunity**. As we grow, however, we also develop or **acquire** immunity to specific pathogens. This involves different cells of the immune system.

Getting to the specifics

Throughout our lifetime we are exposed to many different disease-causing micro-organisms. Over time, it is possible that pathogens such as the flu virus, chickenpox virus and potentially harmful bacteria will find their way into our body. In such circumstances, the body's first lines of defence and phagocytosis may not be able to work efficiently enough. They fail to prevent pathogens spreading through the body fluids and infecting body cells.

If this happens, we rely on the cells of our immune system to carry out a **specific** immune response. This involves other types of **white blood cells** (different from those involved in phagocytosis) called **lymphocytes** (pronounced lim-foe-sites). The process relies on specific **protein** molecules that are present on the surface of the pathogens, called **antigens**.

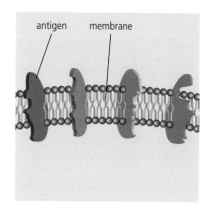

antigen   membrane

Self versus non-self

Tiny proteins called antigens are present on the surface of all your body cells. These are called '**self-antigens**' that are recognised by the cells of the body's immune system as 'belonging' to you. Under normal circumstances, lymphocytes will not attack cells bearing 'self-antigens'. If, however, foreign cells, or pathogens bearing 'non-self' antigens, enter the body, these will be recognised as not belonging to your body and the lymphocytes will begin an immune response.

Lymphocytes – a two-pronged attack

One type of lymphocyte, the **B-lymphocyte**, produces special proteins that will fit exactly to the shape of the antigens on the surface of the pathogen. These proteins are called **antibodies**.

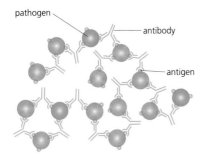

Antibodies are Y-shaped molecules which bind with the pathogens, causing them to become clumped together and immobile. This process is an effective way of preventing the pathogens infecting body cells, as well as making it easier for them to be destroyed.

Once the antibodies have been made, specifically in response to one type of non-self antigen, a few will remain in the body, ready to multiply quickly should the body be re-infected by the same pathogen (or one bearing the same shape of antigens). If this happens, the immune response will be even quicker and more effective – meaning that the person is unlikely to experience any symptoms of illness. So, after the first exposure and response, the body is said to have **acquired immunity**. Your body will remember that you have been exposed to the pathogen before – acquired immunity usually 'remembers' previous infections.

And if invaders get past these barriers...

Should body cells themselves actually be infected by a pathogen, there is another type of lymphocyte, the **T-lymphocyte,** which will respond to overcome the infection. Again, this is a **specific** response to the presence of the non-self antigens.

When a pathogen finds a way inside a body cell, its surface antigens will move onto the surface of the **host** cell. This causes one of the body's own cells to bear non-self antigens! This promotes a response

by the T-lymphocytes to attack the infected body cell with chemicals. The T-lymphocytes divide into **T-helper cells** and **Killer-T cells.**

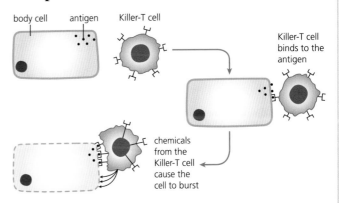

Some of the T-helper cells will remain in the body after the first response, ready to activate the Killer-T cells rapidly, should there be another infection by the same pathogen. This is another example of **acquired immunity**.

QUESTIONS

1 Review all the previous information about how you are protected from infection and create a flow chart to summarise each of the defences.

2 Find out how B-lymphocytes and T-lymphocytes got their names.

3 Find out about the different roles played by T-helper cells and Killer-T cells.

4 Which of the T-lymphocytes do you think are most likely to be sometimes called 'memory cells'?

5 Suggest what might happen to the pathogens that are immobilised by antibodies once they are all 'clumped' together. (Think: how might they be broken down?)

6 Find out ways in which we could help to prevent harmful micro-organisms from entering a cut in the skin. Design a 'First Aid' sign that could deliver this message to the other pupils in your class.

Passive immunity

When the body's immune system defends cells from attack, either by making antibodies or using T-lymphocytes, we describe this as **active** immunity. It's easy to think of it this way because the immune system is becoming active in response to the presence of non-self antigens and begins to manufacture specific proteins and cells to defend the body from disease.

Sometimes, however, there are situations when the body can receive 'ready-made' antibodies. This means that the body itself doesn't need to come in to direct contact with a disease-causing micro-organism. No pathogen means no non-self antigens and, therefore, no hard work for the immune system. This is called **passive** immunity, as the immune system does not have to be active to respond to infection, while the body still **acquires** immunity in the form of ready-made specific antibodies.

Natural versus artificial

The 'ready-made' antibodies must come from somewhere! There are different ways that our body might receive antibodies – some by **natural** means, some by **artificial** means.

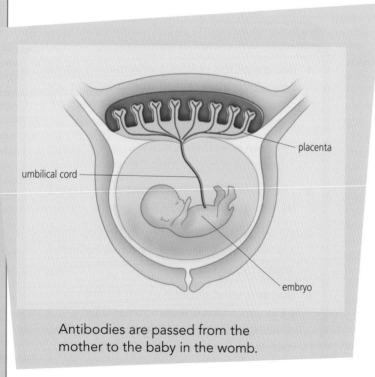

umbilical cord

placenta

embryo

Antibodies are passed from the mother to the baby in the womb.

Antibodies are also passed from the mother to the baby in breast milk.

Antibodies made by humans or animals can be extracted and then introduced artificially to a person's body by injection to provide immunity. This method of acquiring **artificial passive immunity** is sometimes used when infection with the pathogen is likely to cause very unpleasant symptoms of illness and it would be dangerous for the body to have no immunity at all.

Artificial Immunity

Injecting ready-made antibodies is only one way that we can artificially acquire immunity. Many of the **immunisations** that we receive as we grow up involve our immune system being 'provoked' into making an active immune response. This involves **artificially** introducing pathogens into the body that have non-self surface antigens so that our body makes specific anti-bodies.

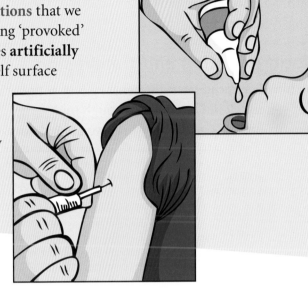

The pathogens contained in **vaccines** are usually weakened in some way or are 'attenuated' so that they don't cause nasty symptoms of the disease.

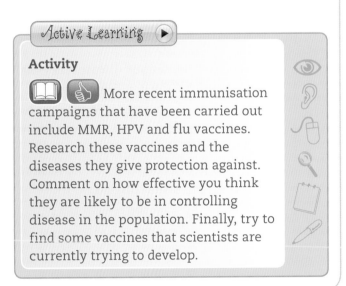

Smallpox – a case study

This disease killed many people throughout Britain until the twentieth century. A doctor called Edward Jenner developed a **vaccine** containing some particles of a similar virus called 'cowpox'. He carried out pioneering experiments infecting people with the pus from cowpox. The cowpox virus was less harmful, but had the same shape of antigens on its surface. When given injections of the cowpox vaccine, a person's immune system would begin an active response, making specific antibodies and acquiring immunity not only to cowpox, but also to the more serious smallpox.

Eventually the disease was completely wiped out, or **eradicated**, in Britain and, more recently, was completely eradicated worldwide, thanks to an effective immunisation programme carried out by the World Health Organisation.

Active Learning ▶

Activity

📖 👍 More recent immunisation campaigns that have been carried out include MMR, HPV and flu vaccines. Research these vaccines and the diseases they give protection against. Comment on how effective you think they are likely to be in controlling disease in the population. Finally, try to find some vaccines that scientists are currently trying to develop.

Too much of a good thing

Surely the immune system is a good thing? It protects our body cells from infection, disease and death. So, surely there can't be too much of a good thing? Well actually…

Sometimes it would be useful for our immune system not to do its job. There are one or two situations when it would be useful if cells of the immune system didn't attack 'non-self' cells.

Blood donation and transfusion

Red blood cells can have different types of antigens on their surface. If someone is seriously ill or suffers a lot of blood loss through injury, they may require to be given a **blood transfusion**. This means they are given blood donated by another person who is healthy.

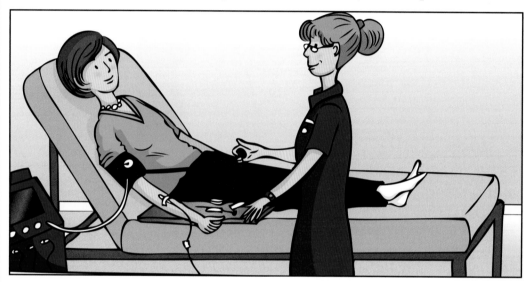

In this situation, if someone is given blood with antigens that don't match the patient, the consequences could be very serious. Antibodies would be produced in response to the 'non-self' antigens and the red blood cells would end up all clumped together. It is important in such circumstances to check that the **blood groups** are the same. This indicates that the surface antigens are the same.

Transplant surgery

When people suffer from serious diseases they may require **transplant surgery**. This is when some tissue or an organ is taken from one human and is placed into the body of another. Since this procedure often involves groups of different cells that carry their own antigen markers, it is a very difficult task to get a complete match. Many tests are carried out to ensure that the antigens on the donor organ are a close match to those on the cells of the patient.

After a transplant operation, a patient will be placed on medication to **suppress** their immune system. This tries to prevent their immune system from attacking the transplanted organ, resulting in **rejection**. While a successful transplant usually has life-saving consequences, the suppression of the person's immune system leaves them vulnerable to different infections and so the patient's recovery is normally very closely monitored by medical staff and can take a long time.

A good thing gone bad

Sometimes the immune system doesn't function the way that it should. It can over-react to harmless things (an **allergic reaction**) or attack the cells of the body (this is called **autoimmune disease**).

Allergic reactions

Many people suffer from allergic reactions to relatively harmless substances. For example, people can have allergies to house dust, plant pollen, animal hair or certain foods such as eggs, wheat or nuts. In these cases, allergic reactions can range from very mild symptoms to very severe, depending on the person. The most severe allergic reaction is called **anaphylaxis**.

An allergic reaction is an over-reaction by the immune system to something which is usually harmless. The B-lymphocytes will begin to produce antibodies which in this case bind to **mast cells** in the body. The presence of the antibodies stimulates the production of a chemical from the mast cells which produces the symptoms we associate with allergic reactions: coughing, sneezing, streaming eyes, itchiness and difficulty breathing.

Autoimmune disease

Sometimes the immune system attacks cells of the body that are 'self'. This might happen if someone has suffered from something like a virus and the immune system has gone into 'over-drive', but **autoimmunity** could also happen without any obvious explanation.

Active Learning ▶

Activity

📖 👍 Two examples of autoimmune diseases are Multiple Sclerosis (MS) and Rheumatoid Arthritis. Research these illnesses and design an electronic presentation or web page that could provide information about the symptoms, causes and treatments of each disease that could be used by a newly diagnosed patient seeking advice.

Life in a bubble

Some children are born with a faulty immune system. Without an immune system any infection, a cold or measles, could be fatal.

Children with a faulty immune system can only survive if they are artificially protected from infection. They live their lives inside a sterile bubble.

The condition they suffer from is called Severe Combined Immune Deficiency disease or SCID. A child with SCID is unable to make the white blood cells that are essential to fight infection.

One possible treatment for this condition is a bone marrow transplant. The bone marrow is where white blood cells are made. Bone marrow is found inside bones. Bone marrow contains **stem cells** that specialise into different blood cell types.

Red marrow bone production in adults

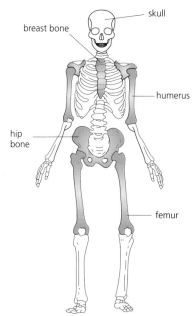

skull
breast bone
humerus
hip bone
femur

Active Learning ▶

Activity

1 Create a memory map to show all the types of cell that contribute to the immune response.

2 The bone marrow register was set up to allow people to donate their bone marrow to people who might need it, such as children with SCID. Would you join the bone marrow register?

3 New treatments for SCID involve the use of stem cells. Find out about stem cells.

4 Would vaccination help children with SCID?

GLOSSARY

Acquire to gain a new property

Allergic reaction body's response to substances to which the individual is sensitive e.g. sneezing and pollen allergy

Anaphylaxis severe allergic reaction requiring urgent medical treatment

Antibody Y-shaped protein involved in the immune response

Antigen a substance that promotes the production of an antibody

Autoimmune disease an immune disease when the body attacks itself

Blood transfusion transferring blood from one person to another

Cilia tiny hair-like structures on the surface of some cells which help move materials away from the cell

Enzyme protein that controls chemical reactions inside the body

Immune response the sequence of co-ordinated responses by the body to attack infections

Immunisation the process of artificially making someone immune to a particular infection

Immunity being immune and able to resist a particular infection

Innate existing since birth –inherited from parents or acquired in the womb

Lymphocyte white blood cell involved in the immune response. There are two types: B-lymphocytes and T-lymphocytes

Lysosome cell organelle which contains enzymes that kill cells

Macrophage white blood cell involved in the immune response

Mast cell cell which releases chemicals and triggers immune response

Micro-organism a tiny living thing

Mucus protective liquid found in the mouth, nose and other body openings

Pathogen a disease-causing organism

Phagocyte white blood cell involved in the immune response

Stem cell cell that is capable of reproducing and specialising in a number of different ways

Vaccine living or dead micro-organisms which are used to give artificial immunity

BIOLOGICAL SYSTEMS

Inheritance

12

Fertilisation

Level 2 — What came before?

 SCN 2-14a

By investigating the lifecycles of plants and animals, I can recognise the different stages of their development.

Level 3 — What is this chapter about?

 SCN 3-14a

I understand the process of fertilisation and embryonic development and can discuss possible risks to the embryo.

Fertilisation

The moment of fertilisation, when a new life is made, is called *conception*, which means *beginning*.

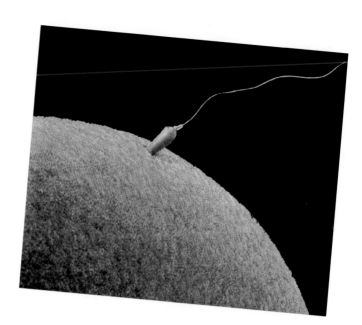

'In vitro' fertilization (IVF)

'**In vitro**' means '*in glass*'. Louise Brown made the news headlines when she was born on 25 July 1978.

Louise was conceived in a glass tube using sperm cells from her father and an egg from one of her mother's ovaries. 60 hours later, doctors implanted that newly-conceived life into Louise's mother's uterus and the fertilised egg then developed normally until she was born.

The technique was termed *in vitro* fertilization – **IVF**. Louise's life was the first human life to begin outside the human body.

IVF was required because Louise's mother's **fallopian tubes** were blocked which prevented her eggs reaching her womb. The doctors used IVF to by-pass the damaged fallopian tube.

In vivo fertilisation

In vivo means '*within the living*'; in other words the way that things happen in nature.

Sex cells are called **gametes**. The human sex cells, **sperm** and **ova**, join together at **fertilisation**. The fertilised egg is known as a **zygote**.

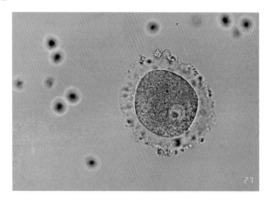

The process of converting a fertilised ovum into a baby requires a complex plan which is contained within the **DNA**. All of the cells of the developing offspring contain all of the **genes**. Genes are turned on and off to allow different types of tissues to develop.

A zygote divides into two cells; these then grow and divide into four, then eight, sixteen and so on until the cells are too numerous to count and they develop into different tissues.

Where do female gametes come from?

Female gametes, ova, are made in the ovaries which are part of the female reproductive system.

The ovum is quite a large cell and includes a food store. Generally once every 28 days, from puberty to menopause, one ovum is released from an ovary. This process is termed ovulation.

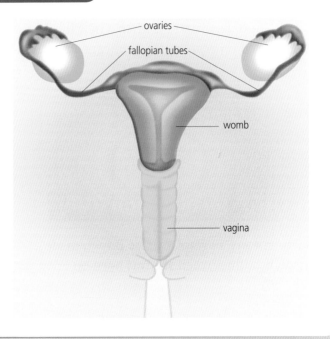

The ovum is captured by the fringes of the fallopian tubes. The fallopian tubes are lined with beating hair-like **cilia** (pronounced Sill-i-a) which sweep the ovum towards the uterus.

Where do male gametes come from?

Male gametes are made in the **testes** (pronounced test-ees) which are part of the male reproductive system. Huge numbers of sperm cells are made in the testes.

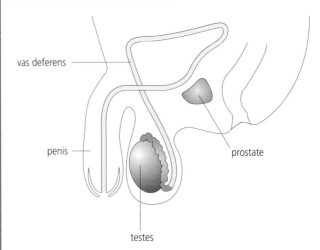

It has been estimated that as many as 100 million (100 000 000) sperm cells are made in the testes every day after puberty.

Where do male gametes come from?

The sperm are small cells that are nourished by fluid added from the prostate and Cowper's glands. The tail allows the sperm to swim towards the ovum along the fallopian tubes. Sperms are attracted to the ovum by chemicals.

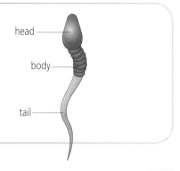

Fertilisation is a race against time

Following sexual intercourse as many as 300 million sperm cells compete on the journey to reach one egg. Not many of them reach the fallopian tube.

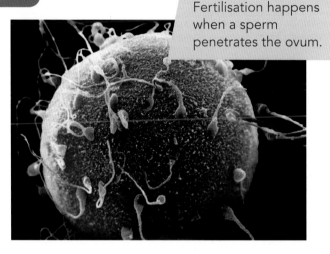

Fertilisation happens when a sperm penetrates the ovum.

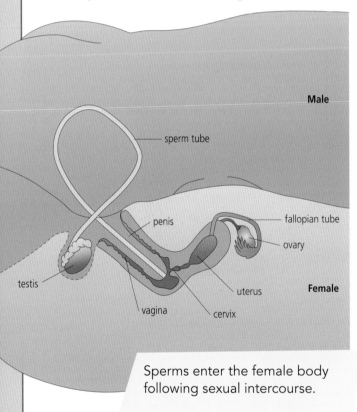

Male

sperm tube

penis

fallopian tube

ovary

testis

uterus   Female

vagina   cervix

Sperms enter the female body following sexual intercourse.

The term conception is also used to describe fertilisation. Sperm contains half the genetic material required to begin a new life (the other half is contained in the ovum)

The fertilised ovum is now termed a **zygote**. The zygote will then start to grow and divide into two cells

Identical twins result when the zygote separates into two after cell division has occurred. Non-identical twins arise from the production and fertilisation of two eggs by two different sperm.

An unfertilised ovum will only live for about 18 to 24 hours in the fallopian tube. Sperm cells can survive in the fluids of the female reproductive system for up to 3 days. It takes sperm cells about 10 hours to swim from the vagina through the cervix, and into the fallopian tube. Although 300 million sperm may enter the upper part of the vagina, only 1%, 3 million, enter the uterus and swim on towards the fallopian tube.

From fertilisation to birth

The zygote, which at this stage is made of only one cell, now divides to form two genetically identical cells, the two cells become four, four become eight and this process is repeated until there is a ball of cells, no bigger than the original cell.

The dividing zygote continues to get propelled along the fallopian tube by the movements of the cilia towards the uterus. Approximately four days after fertilisation, the zygote is composed of approximately 100 cells and is called a **blastocyst**.

Between five and eight days after fertilisation, the blastocyst attaches to the lining of the uterus. This process is termed implantation. Cells found within the blastocyst develop into the **embryo**, while cells on the outer layer become embedded in the wall of the uterus and eventually form the **placenta**.

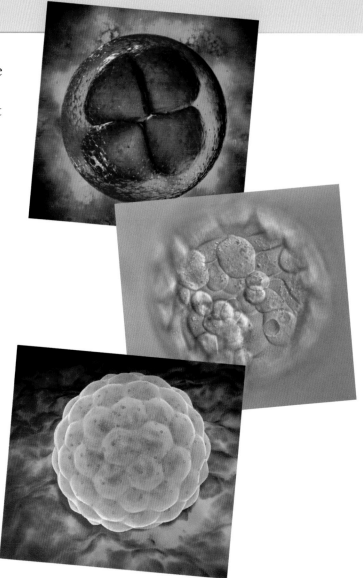

The placenta carries oxygen and nutrients from the mother to the embryo. The placenta also removes waste materials, including carbon dioxide and urea, away from the embryo. The placenta also provides a barrier which prevents embryonic and maternal blood coming into direct contact.

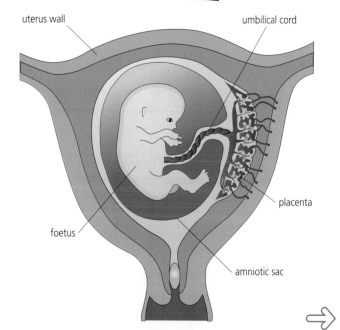

uterus wall

umbilical cord

placenta

foetus

amniotic sac

The cells of the amniotic sac develop by day 12. This sac fills with liquid which cushions the developing embryo inside the uterus.

The formation of most of the internal organs and external body structures takes place during the embryonic stage. The embryo becomes longer and different tissues start to develop.

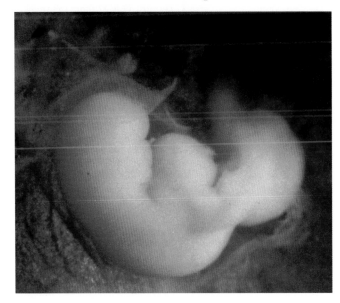

By the end of the 8th week after fertilisation the embryo is considered to be a **foetus** (pronounced feet-us).

By 24 weeks of pregnancy the foetus has a chance of survival outside the uterus. With improving medical support this time scale is reducing slightly.

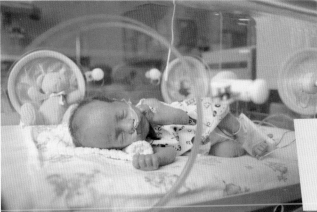

Elizabeth was 1.4 kg when she was born at 32 weeks. This was 8 (40–32) weeks premature.

The placenta is fully formed by 18 to 20 weeks but continues to grow throughout pregnancy.

QUESTIONS

1 Arrange the following terms into the correct sequence to describe the increasing number of cells:

New born baby, Blastocyst, Ovum, Embryo, Zygote, Foetus.

2 Prepare a table that compares human gametes – the ovum with the sperms. Use the following headings:

a) size

b) food store

c) movement.

3 Write a sentence to explain the function of each of the following:

a) the placenta

b) amniotic fluid

c) the umbilical cord

d) fallopian tubes

e) cilia.

Summary of human development

Length: 0.1–0.15 mm (1 day after ovulation)
Fertilisation begins when a sperm penetrates an ovum and is completed when the ovum becomes a zygote.

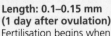

Length: 0.1–0.2 mm (3 days after ovulation)
The zygote now begins to divide, each division occurring approximately every 20 hours. The cells become smaller but more numerous. The ball of cells leaves the fallopian tube and enters the uterus 3 to 4 days after fertilisation.

Length: 0.1–0.2 mm (4 days after ovulation)
The ball of cells develops a central cavity and is now called a blastocyst.

Length: 0.1–0.2 mm (5 to 6 days after ovulation)
The blastocyst settles into the wall of the uterus and the process of implantation begins. The uterus becomes swollen with new blood capillaries and the circulation between mother and blastocyst begin to develop. Hormones are released from the ovary to maintain the placenta and to prevent the release of more ova.

Length: 0.2 mm (13 days after ovulation)
The placenta begins to develop. The embryo divides into three layers from which all tissues and organs will develop. This is a critical stage in the development. The embryo is at greatest risk at this stage.

Length: 1.5–3.0 mm (21 to 23 days after ovulation)
Rapid cell growth during this stage. The heart starts to beat.

Length: 2.5–3.0 mm (23 to 25 days after ovulation)
The central nervous system is the most developed system at this stage.

Length: 4.0–6.0 mm (26 to 30 days after ovulation)
Cells which will become the digestive system start to appear.

Length: 5.0–7.0 mm (31 to 35 days after ovulation)
Valves begin to form in the heart.

Length: 7.0–9.0 mm (35 to 38 days after ovulation)
The brain has greatly increased in size and remains larger than the rest of the body. Kidneys begin to develop.

Length: 9.0–11.0 mm (38 to 42 days after ovulation)
The part of the brain which is responsible for heart, breathing and muscle movements, begins to develop.
The lower jaw starts to be formed.

Length: 10.0–13.0mm (42 to 44 days after ovulation)
Teeth buds begin to form. Trachea, bronchi and diaphragm begin to form. The heart begins to separate into its four chambers.

Length: 11.0–14.0mm (44 to 48 days after ovulation)
Kidneys begin to produce urine for the first time. Bone cell formation of the skeleton begins

Length: 13.0–18.0mm (48 to 51 days after ovulation)
The sex organs begin to form. Toenails begin to appear.

Length: 15.0–20.0mm (51 to 53 days after ovulation)
Brain is connected to muscles and nerves. As a result the embryo can make some movements. Testes or ovaries can be seen and the sex of the embryo can be determined.

Length: 17.0–22.0mm (53 to 54 days after ovulation)
Tongue development is complete. Intestines are now becoming organised.

Length: 19.0–24.0mm (54 to 56 days after ovulation)
Cartilage begins to be replaced by bone. The fingers are seen to be separate. The embryo still has a stubby tail but this is becoming smaller.

Length: 23.0–26.0mm (56 to 60 days after ovulation)
This is the end of the embryonic phase of development as the embryo has become recognisably human and is now termed a **foetus**. Taste buds begin to form on the surface of the tongue. Upper and lower limbs are well formed. The toes are no longer webbed and the tail has disappeared.

Length: 31– 42mm (10 weeks after ovulation)
Basic brain structure of the foetus is complete and now the brain mass rapidly increases. Face has human appearance. Vocal cords form. Intestines are now located in the abdomen.

Muscles of the digestive system can contract. The liver starts to produce bile. Fingernails begin to grow.

Length: 61mm (12 weeks after ovulation) Mass: between 8 to 14 g
Foetus begins to move around. Heartbeat can be detected with a stethoscope. Lungs develop further as the foetus inhales and exhales amniotic fluid. Body hair begins to grow.

While you read this section we suggest you sit with a ruler and a set of scales in front of you. Add sand to the scales to match the masses indicated in the text.

Length: 21cm (24 weeks after ovulation) Mass: 540 g

Blood vessels develop in the lungs to allow the foetus to breathe air after birth. The air sacs begin to produce a chemical known as surfactant. This liquid stops the membranes of the air sacs from sticking together and the air sacs from being unable to inflate.

Length: 23cm (26 weeks after ovulation) Mass 910 g

Lungs are capable of breathing air. The testes of the male foetus have fully descended from their position in the abdomen and are now located in the scrotal sacs.

40 weeks after ovulation

The foetus at this stage is considered to be 'full term'.

Length: 38cm (40 weeks after ovulation) Mass: 3.4 kg

By this stage 15% of the total mass of the body is made of fat. At birth, the baby has 300 bones. Some of these bones fuse together at a later date to form a total of 206 bones found in an adult human.

Length: 19cm (20 weeks after ovulation) Mass 350 g

Bones of the ear harden, allowing the foetus to detect sound. By 21 weeks, the foetal bone marrow starts making blood cells. This was previously done by the liver and spleen.

Length: 25cm (28 weeks after ovulation) Mass: 1.1 kg

Head hair has developed. The bone marrow now produces red blood cells. A layer of insulating fat which has been deposited under the skin causes the skin to become less wrinkled. It is also a food store.

Length 14–16cm (18 weeks after ovulation) Mass 260 g

Testes move down from the pelvis into the scrotum. Skeleton hardens.

Length: 108–111mm (16 weeks after ovulation) Mass: 80 g

Approximately 250 ml of amniotic fluid surrounds the foetus at this time. The blinking reflex develops. Fingerprints and toe prints develop. Vernix covers the skin. The vernix is made of dead skin and oil produced by the foetus.

Length: 27cm (30 weeks after ovulation) Mass: 1.35 kg

The brain continues to grow rapidly. The foetus is confined by lack of space in the uterus and its legs are tucked up into the foetal position.

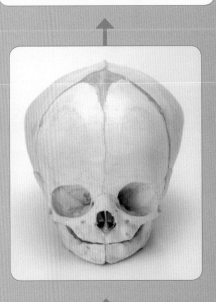

Length: 35cm (38 weeks after ovulation) Mass: 3.1 kg

The skull is not yet solid. Soft spots, **fontanelles**, allow the skull to move during birth without damaging the brain of the foetus.

Length: 80–90mm (14 weeks after ovulation) Mass: 25 g

The heart pumps about 25 litres of blood per day. The body now grows rapidly.

Length: 29cm (32weeks after ovulation) Mass 1.8 kg

Foetus begins to develop its own immune system which will provide defence against disease. Foetus has until now been defended by mother's immunity.

Length: 32cm (34 weeks after ovulation) Mass 2.28 kg

Gravity generally causes the foetus to move into the head-down delivery position in the pelvis.

Length: 34cm (36 weeks after ovulation) Mass: 2.75 kg

Body is round and plump with new fat. Fat storage continues to develop. Hardening of the flexible bones continues. Foetal movements are limited by lack of space.

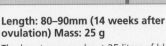

A bouncing baby!

Babies generally have blue eyes at birth because the pigments in the iris are not fully developed. Full iris pigmentation usually occurs during the first weeks after birth as it requires the eyes to be exposed to light.

Babies are born with more than 70 instinctive (pre-programmed and unlearned) behaviour patterns e.g. suckling response for feeding. This aids survival.

Learned behaviour develops throughout the remainder of the individual's life.

Have you been vaccinated with the rubella vaccine?

Rubella (German measles) is a mild condition for most adults and teenagers. However, rubella causes serious damage to unborn babies. It can affect the baby's growth, heart, vision, hearing and brain development.

In the UK the rubella vaccine is contained in a combination vaccine called MMR (measles, mumps and rubella). The MMR vaccine is given as a series of two doses at 12 to 15 months of age and at 4 to 6 years of age.

QUESTIONS

1   a)   List as many human instincts as you can think of.

b)   List 10 examples of learned behaviour.

Timeline of Rubella (German measles) showing 5 stages:

1752	discovered by a German doctor
1866	named rubella by a Scottish doctor
1941	birth defects e.g. cataracts and blindness, linked to rubella by Australian eye surgeon
1963	to 1965 worldwide epidemic rubella viruses infected estimated 10% of all pregnant women, and 30% of their infants developed problems
1969	rubella virus was grown in a laboratory and identified as being responsible for the disease. First vaccine produced that year

If you have been immunised, you are protected from rubella infection. Pregnant women who have been vaccinated protect their unborn children being exposed to rubella.

$\Longrightarrow$

The rubella virus is one of a wide variety of agents which may affect the developing human embryo or **foetus**.

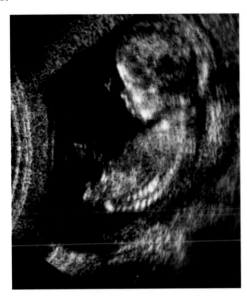

The foetus in the uterus is not completely protected from the outside world and is influenced by lots of external influences. **Teratogens** are factors that can cause birth defects in a developing embryo or foetus.

Teratogens

The scientific study of embryo/foetal abnormalities caused by external agents is known as teratology.

Teratogens are agents or factors that can cause birth defects in a developing embryo or foetus.

Rubella is a teratogen and its effects are said to be teratogenic.

It has been estimated that approximately 1 in 33 babies are born with birth defects. Birth defects can be caused by either genetic or environmental factors. Teratogens are an example of environmental factors that lead to birth defects.

Many birth defects caused by teratogens are preventable.

The vast majority of women in UK have uncomplicated pregnancies and give birth to healthy infants.

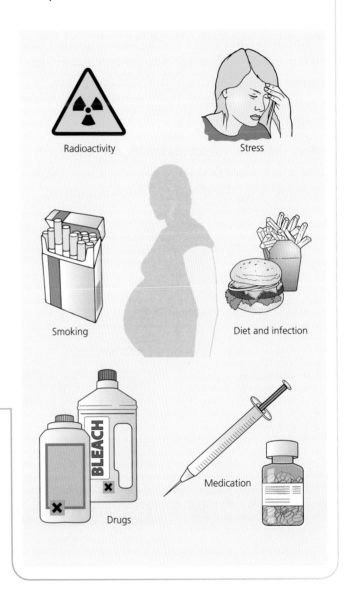

Radioactivity

Stress

Smoking

Diet and infection

BLEACH

Drugs

Medication

The severity of the teratogen's effects vary depending, for example, on the type of agent, extent of maternal exposure to the agent, rate of teratogen absorption and placental transfer, stage of development of the foetus and the **genotype** of the mother and offspring.

$\Rightarrow$

Teratogens

Different teratogens affect developing cells and tissues in various ways. Abnormal development results in death, growth inhibition or disorders of body structure or function.

Teratogens can cause changes to DNA which result in chromosome damage. Chromosome damage causes mutations which means that cells are changed. These changes lead to problems in the foetus.

More than 600 suspected teratogens have been identified. The effects of a few dozen have been documented. Much more research is required.

Teratogens can be grouped into four main groups:

- Chemical agents
- Infectious agents
- Physical agents
- Maternal conditions.

Chemical teratogens can affect a baby in the womb

Chemical teratogens include pollutants, medicines and recreational 'drugs'.

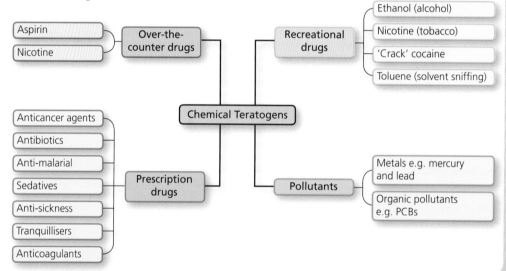

Case study: A prescription drug

Thalidomide (pronounced Tha-lid-o-mide) was a drug sold from 1957 until the early 1960s to combat morning sickness in pregnant women. It was discovered that thalidomide was a teratogen which resulted in severe birth defects in babies born to women who had taken the drug.

Thalidomide affects foetal development. Approximately 15 000 foetuses were damaged by Thalidomide. In total, 12 000 children from 46 countries were born with significant birth defects caused by Thalidomide. Four thousand of them died during their first year of life.

Although Thalidomide was banned for use against morning sickness it is being tested for use in the treatment of leprosy, HIV and prostate cancer.

Case study: A recreational drug

Research scientists have shown that the foetus is affected by cigarette smoking during pregnancy.

Smoking tobacco increases the risk of bleeding, early breaking of the amniotic sac, miscarriage and deaths of new born babies. Women who smoke during pregnancy give birth to babies who are around 225 grams lighter and smaller than babies born to non-smokers (average birth weight is 3.4 kg). These babies may be more likely to be born prematurely and have other health problems.

Infective teratogens can affect a baby in the womb

Infections may attack the unborn baby in the womb or during birth. Infections at any time during pregnancy may affect growth, damage part of the foetus or cause death.

The placenta cannot act as a barrier to all diseases. Infants may be born suffering from the effects of infections, e.g. malaria, measles, chicken pox, mumps, syphilis and other sexually transmitted diseases.

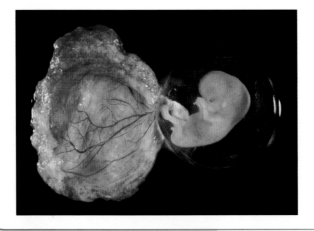

Early diagnosis, effective treatments and infection prevention strategies are required to minimise the effects of infections.

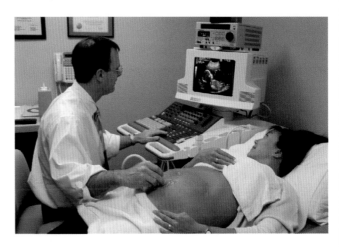

Many micro-organisms are known to be teratogens. Virus diseases such as rubella, chicken pox, measles and HIV are able to pass across the placenta. Several bacterial and protozoan diseases are also able to infect unborn babies.

Case study: mumps – a viral disease

Mumps is a virus that causes swelling in the salivary glands, which lasts about a week. Patients should be isolated to prevent the spread of the infection, especially to pregnant women. Mumps during pregnancy sometimes results in miscarriage or even the death of the foetus. Mumps immunisation is part of the MMR vaccine.

Case study: Listeria – a bacterial disease

Listeria is a bacterium that contaminates certain foods and can cause problems for the unborn baby. Pregnant women are 20 times more likely to become infected by *Listeria* than other adults. Symptoms similar to flu appear 2–30 days after eating contaminated food.

Miscarriage, premature birth and infection to the newborn may result from *Listeria* exposure. Around 20% of *Listeria* infections in the womb result in death of the foetus. Early treatment with antibiotics may prevent foetal infection and foetal death.

Pasteurisation and cooking destroys *Listeria* bacteria.

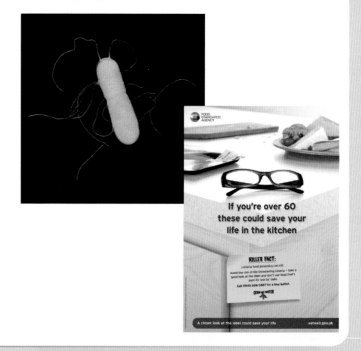

Physical teratogens can affect a baby in the womb

Sometimes the physical conditions inside the womb can affect foetal growth. Mechanical forces can place pressure on the foetus and result in deformities e.g. dislocation of the hip.

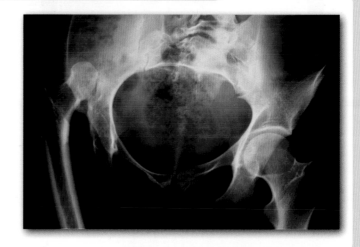

Case study: radiation

Exposure of the foetus to radiation can result in mutations and death. Defects may be passed on to the next generation.

The full impact of the world's biggest nuclear accident in Chernobyl, Ukraine, in 1986 may not be known for several generations.

Maternal teratogens can affect a baby in the womb

A mother's health contributes to the health of the unborn offspring. The correct levels of food and oxygen are needed to ensure proper growth and development. Other chemicals can pass across the placenta and enter the foetal bloodstream.

Case study: Dietary iron (Fe)

A nutritious diet during pregnancy is essential for both the mother and the baby. Malnutrition and starvation are major issues in many parts of the world. Lack of iron in the mother's diet will result in anaemia in the foetus and lead to heart and circulatory problems. Iron tablets taken by the mother during pregnancy assist the formation of new blood cells in both the mother and the baby.

Finding out more about teratogens

Teratogenic risks are not fully understood and more scientific research is required.

Records of human births are used to study the effects of possible teratogens. *In vivo* animal experiments are used as well. Animal testing is controversial and controlled by the government.

'We are responsible for the efficient and effective operation of the Animals (Scientific Procedures) Act 1986. Parliament has built in considerable safeguards to allow experimentation in limited circumstances and to ensure proper regulation and monitoring. In carrying out our duties we aim to maintain the balance required by the 1986 Act between the interests of science and industry and animal welfare.'

I am against animal experiments because they cause suffering to animals. The benefits to human beings have not been proved. Any benefits could be produced in other ways.

I am in favour of animal experiments as long as suffering is minimised in all experiments. The benefits to humans of experiments on animals could not be obtained by other methods.

Spare a thought for infertile couples on Mother's and Father's Days

When you see shops filled with gifts and cards for Mother's and Father's Days it is worth remembering that an estimated 1 750 000 couples in the UK (one in seven) may be experiencing the stress and anxiety of trying to conceive.

In vitro fertilisation (IVF) and intrauterine insemination techniques have been developed to assist with conception.

We've brought medical experts and the latest IVF treatments from all over the **world.**

Because we know this treatment means the **world** to you.

IVF
scotland

To make an appointment
call 0131 6545680

IVF Scotland, a subsidiary of the Spire Healthcare hospital network is here to help individuals and couples who are having difficulty conceiving.

The Human Fertilisation and Embryology Authority (HFEA) is the UK's independent regulator overseeing the use of gametes and embryos in fertility treatment and research. The HFEA licenses fertility clinics and centres carrying out IVF, other assisted conception procedures and human embryo research.

The HFEA has warned that children conceived artificially through IVF may have a 30% higher risk of genetic abnormalities.

Research has found that IVF babies suffer increased rates of heart valve defects, cleft lip and palate and digestive system abnormalities due to the bowel or oesophagus failing to form properly.

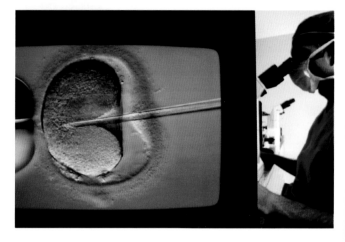

A complication of 'infertility treatment' is the risk of multiple births.

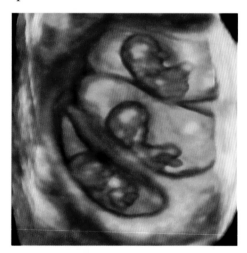

Babies resulting from multiple pregnancies tend to be born prematurely and demonstrate a significantly increased risk of ill health.

In the UK, the HFEA has introduced limits to the number of embryos that can be implanted during fertility treatment and this is normally two.

GLOSSARY

Blastocyst a ball of cells formed by the repeated division of a zygote

Cilia tiny hair-like structures on the surface of some cells which help move materials away from the cell

DNA the chemical that transfers genetic information between living things

Embryo a living thing in the early stages of development

Fallopian tube (oviduct) tube that carries ova from the ovaries to the womb (uterus)

Fertilisation process that takes place when gametes join together to make a zygote e.g. sperm fertilises ovum and pollen fertilises ovules

Foetus an unborn mammal with strong similarity to the appearance of its species – in humans 8 weeks after fertilisation

Fontanelle spaces between the bones of a new born baby's head

Gamete sex cells – sperm and ova

Gene basic unit of inheritance that codes for protein formation

Genotype the genetic information contained in an individual's DNA

In vitro a biological experiment that takes place in a container

In vivo a biological experiment or process that takes place inside the living thing

Ova (Plural, singular ovum) female gamete

Placenta organ in most female mammals which serves to supply food and oxygen and remove waste from a developing embryo/foetus

Sperm male gamete

Testes male sex organ which produces sperm

Teratogens agents that cause birth defects in the womb

Zygote product of fertilisation

BIOLOGICAL SYSTEMS

Inheritance

13

DNAzing!

Level 2   What came before?

 SCN 2-14b

By exploring the characteristics offspring inherit when living things reproduce, I can distinguish between inherited and non-inherited characteristics.

Level 3   What is this chapter about?

 SCN 3-14b

I have extracted DNA and understand its function. I can express an informed view of the risks and benefits of DNA profiling.

DNAzing!

DNA is amazing! Its discovery and extraction has lead to advances in medical science, agriculture, **forensic** science, and our scientific understanding even led to the creation of 'Dolly the Sheep'.

Where is DNA?

DNA is found in all living things. It is mainly found in the cell nucleus.

Dolly the 'Celebrity' Sheep, made in Scotland, was the World's first **cloned** mammal made from an adult cell.

Extracting DNA

You can extract the DNA from fruit and vegetables. This is really very simple. It did, however, take scientists a long time to figure out how to get samples of DNA.

Take a Kiwi fruit, onion or strawberry – or try your own choice of fruit or vegetable (animal tissues work as well but they are a lot messier to work with).

Cut it into small pieces and then mush it up with warm salty water for 5 to 10 seconds.
This helps to break up the cells.

Pour the liquid through a coffee filter into a boiling tube.
This helps to remove large lumps and separate it from cellular material and sap.

Gently stir in 2 tsp of household detergent. (Be very gentle and **do not** make bubbles.)
The detergent breaks up cell membranes as well as the nuclear membrane so that the DNA will be released into the extract.

Slowly pour chilled alcohol down the side of the boiling tube so that it remains as a separate level on top of the treated fruit extract.

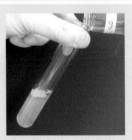

Leave it for 5 to 10 minutes and you should then see the DNA appear as a layer of 'gloopy' material between the two liquid layers.

What is DNA?

DNA is found in living things and contains just a few chemical elements – carbon, hydrogen, oxygen, nitrogen and phosphorus (C, H, O, N and P).

DNA is the short version of a really long name. Impress your friends by saying 'de-oxy-ribo-new-clay-ic acid'.

Genes are made from **DNA** and they code for our appearance e.g. eye colour. They also control things that we can do e.g. digest our food.

DNA contains the chemical code for all **genetic** information, the instructions to make new living things.

Chromosomes are made of thousands of genes, joined together in a particular order.

DNA is found in every cell nucleus in our body and almost every cell in every living thing.

You have 46 chromosomes arranged in 23 pairs containing 30 000 genes between them.

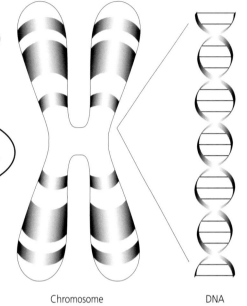

Chromosome   DNA

Chromosome complement

All living organisms, including plants and animals, have a characteristic number of **chromosomes**, called the **chromosome complement**. It may surprise you to learn that horses have 66 chromosomes, compared with 46 in humans and 8 in onions. Although they are each different species, the chromosomes are all made of thousands of genes, which in turn are all made of the same chemical, DNA. You may be wondering how it is that a horse is so different to an onion or a human if they all contain DNA; however, it is the DNA code that varies so much between them.

How does the DNA code vary between humans? All humans look fairly similar in many ways and resemble close members of family. However, although similar, no two humans have exactly the same DNA, apart from identical twins, who have a matching DNA code.

Activity

Find out each of the following:

- How are identical twins created?

- How similar is the DNA between non-identical twins?

- How similar is the DNA between individual **siblings**?

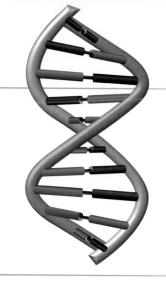

What does DNA look like?

All chemicals, even big ones like DNA, are so small that we cannot see them without complicated scientific equipment.

One of the most exciting breakthroughs of the twentieth century was the discovery of the structure of DNA after studying **X-ray diffraction** photographs taken by **Rosalind Franklin**. Three scientists won the **Nobel Prize** – James Watson, Francis Crick and Maurice Wilkins for describing DNA as a double **helix** structure. It looks just like a ladder that has been twisted into a spiral.

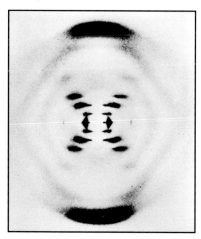

Looking a bit more closely

Each 'rung' of the ladder is held together by a pair of **nucleotide bases**; A is always paired with T; G is always paired with C.

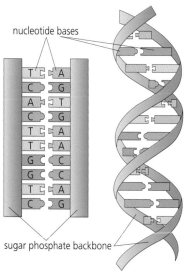

The genetic code

The **genetic code** refers to the exact sequence of bases as they are organised along one strand of DNA. The sequence carries the genetic map for the entire organism. It contains the plan for everything about the living thing – the shape, number and organisation of the cells; whether it will become bacteria, an oak tree or a human. This sequence is copied in every cell of your body and while you will carry lots of genes which you have inherited from your parents, you are different from each of them and you are different from your brothers and sisters (unless you are an identical twin).

Oak tree

Human being

Bacteria

Base sequences

GTAAAGCGGAGCGGCTGCAGCCTGCTGTTGAGTGAGAAAACAAAATTATCTTCCTTTCCA

This is the first line of the sequence of bases in a gene which scientists are studying and which is involved in muscular dystrophy which is an inherited disease. There are 122 other lines of bases for this gene; there are hundreds of other genes on this chromosome.

⊞ Big numbers

The human genome includes around 3 billion bases. (That's 3 000 000 000!)

Use your calculator to find out how many books you would need to contain this information if you have 3 billion bases, 1000 bases per page and 1000 pages in each book.

Calculate the length of the bookshelves you would need if each book measured 10 cm in width.

DNA profiling

All the different techniques that exist for looking at DNA depend on creating small fragments of DNA, and comparing the base sequences. **DNA Profiling**, often called **DNA fingerprinting**, is a technique with wide ranging applications in medicine, scientific research and forensic science.

Restriction enzymes cut DNA into smaller pieces e.g.

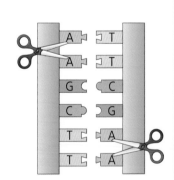

The mechanisms involve cutting DNA with a **restriction enzyme** and carrying out a technique called **electrophoresis**.

Different restriction enzymes can cut DNA into different smaller pieces. These can be used for identification purposes and for further experiments.

Electrophoresis

Many chemicals have small electrical charges. When they are placed in an electrical field, positively charged particles will move towards a negative terminal; negatively charged ones will move towards a positive terminal. Restriction enzymes cut DNA into sequences of different lengths (and, therefore, different numbers of bases). These short sequences of DNA are all electrically charged.

Agarose gel provides a medium through which gel electrophoresis is carried out. This works in much the same way as chromatography, but it relies on the electrically charged molecules moving through the gel at different rates because of their different sizes.

Each gel includes wells into which tiny volumes of DNA are placed. As fragments have been made with restriction enzymes, the DNA will be made up of differently sized particles.

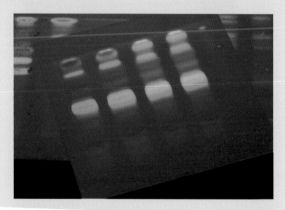

Active Learning

Activity

Find out more about:

- Nobel Prizes
- Rosalind Franklin
- Sir Alec Jeffreys

The discovery of the structure of DNA has given scientists an understanding of the way that living things work, grow and develop. This knowledge is allowing scientists to help cure diseases, make new medicines and understand our connection with all living organisms. Molecular biology and genetics are two branches of science that have grown since the discovery of the structure of DNA.

QUESTIONS

1 Explain why each of the following helps the extraction of DNA from fruit:

   a) 'mushing' the fruit in warm salty water

   b) pouring the liquid through a strainer

   c) stirring in detergent

   d) pouring alcohol down the side of the boiling tube.

2 Use the following terms to complete each of the following sentences: chromosomes, genes, DNA, helix, sugar-phosphate, nucleotide bases:

   a) The chemical code for all living things is contained within a chemical called ____ .

   b) Humans have 46 ____ , 23 pairs which include all the ____ in a particular sequence.

   c) The backbone of DNA is held together by two supporting ____ strands.

   d) DNA is a spiral molecule with two strands. Its discoverers, Crick and Watson, described it as a double ____ .

   e) DNA always has the same amounts of A and T and G and C. These chemicals are ____ which contain the genetic code.

Case study: DNA and the Human Genome Project

Scientists working on the Human Genome Project have created a map that shows the exact location of every gene on human chromosomes. Scientists hope that this understanding will help improve human health, by fixing faulty genes that pass on diseases such as **cystic fibrosis** and certain cancers.

What is the Human Genome Project?

'The Human Genome Project is the largest international collaboration ever undertaken in biology. Between 1990 and 2003, thousands of scientists worldwide undertook the immense task of sequencing the 3 billion bases of genetic information that resides in every human cell.' (The Wellcome Trust)

'Begun formally in 1990, the U.S. Human Genome Project was a 13-year effort co-ordinated by the U.S. Department of Energy and the National Institutes of Health. The project originally was planned to last 15 years, but rapid technological advances accelerated the completion date to 2003.

Project goals were to:

- identify all the approximately 20 000–25 000 genes in human DNA
- determine the sequences of the 3 billion chemical base pairs that make up human DNA
- store this information in databases
- improve tools for data analysis
- transfer related technologies to the private sector, and
- address the ethical, legal and social issues that may arise from the project.'

(The US Department of Energy Office of Science)

Case study: DNA and medical science

Cancer

In order to grow, repair and reproduce, all cells must make copies of themselves. During cell division, the DNA within each cell makes an exact copy of itself, to produce a new cell with a complete set of genetic instructions. Cancers are caused when this process does not work properly. Many different cancers exist.

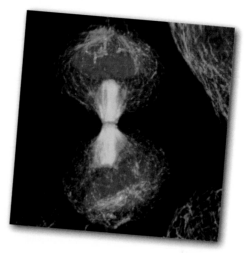

Our cells are constantly replacing themselves, e.g.

- cuts and grazes are quickly replaced with new cells
- our growth since we were children has involved the appearance of new cells
- lots of our skin cells are continuously being shed and form a large proportion of house dust.

The instructions in a cell that tell it **when** to divide and **what** type of cell to become are held within the DNA. DNA is a unique substance in its ability to reproduce itself exactly, in a process called **DNA replication**.

However, whenever a copy is being made, there is a chance that something can go wrong and occasionally the DNA can become damaged or **mutate**.

$\Rightarrow$

Cells can sometimes divide uncontrollably leading to a mass of cells. An abnormal lump forms which is known as a **tumour**. Why and how can cells divide uncontrollably to cause cancer?

Many causes of cancer have been identified e.g. chemicals and radiation but most cancers are the result of damage or defects to the genes that control cell division.

The discovery of the structure of DNA was of massive significance to cancer research, as it helped scientists understand its role in controlling cells and, therefore, cell division.

Case study: DNA and medical science

Gene therapy

Cancer is a disease which is caused by damage to DNA and often develops within a person's lifetime. However, other people are born with inherited damaged DNA, in the form of genetically inherited diseases, such as cystic fibrosis. Through **gene therapy** it is hoped that scientists will be able to remove faulty genes from chromosomes and replace them with a normal copy, to repair the damage to the DNA and help prevent people suffering from certain cancers or genetically inherited diseases.

'Designer' babies

Now that we know the location of certain genes on chromosomes, it is possible that in the near future, people will be able to pick the appearance of their babies by selecting for or against certain genes, including the sex and the colour of eyes and hair.

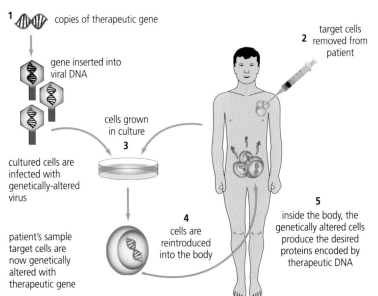

1 copies of therapeutic gene

gene inserted into viral DNA

2 target cells removed from patient

cells grown in culture
3

cultured cells are infected with genetically-altered virus

patient's sample target cells are now genetically altered with therapeutic gene

4 cells are reintroduced into the body

5 inside the body, the genetically altered cells produce the desired proteins encoded by therapeutic DNA

Have your say!

1 What is your opinion on replacing genes in the way described for inherited conditions?

2 What is your opinion on 'designer' babies?

Case study: DNA and animal cloning?

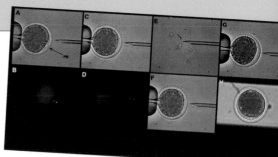

The first mammal to be successfully cloned was Dolly the sheep, born on 5 July 1996 at the Roslin Institute in Edinburgh by **somatic cell nuclear transfer**. Many other animals and animal species have been cloned since that time.

Dolly was cloned from an adult udder cell (mammary gland) from an ewe. An egg cell was removed from another ewe and had its nucleus removed, to get rid of its original set of genetic instructions. The nucleus from the adult udder cell was then inserted into the egg and subjected to an electric current to make it divide into a blastocyst and then implanted into a surrogate mother ewe. Dolly, the most famous and controversial sheep in the world, lived until she was six years old. Her remains are on display at the Royal Museum of Scotland.

Given that we have the human genetic sequence, some people worry that it will only be a matter of time before humans are cloned. This sounds like science fiction, but the creation of Dolly sparked controversy the world over, as many people are opposed to cloning on the basis that they believe it is morally and ethically wrong.

Human therapeutic cloning

Scientists are currently working on therapeutic human cloning to develop clones of human cells to help produce replacement cells for people suffering from conditions such as Alzheimer's and Parkinson's disease; replacement tissue such as skin, for grafts; and organs for organ replacement surgery. The new cloned, 'normal' cells can be injected into the target organ of the sufferer. In the case of Alzhiemer's, into the brain of the patient to encourage the growth of normal healthy brain cells, or the skin can be grafted onto the skin of a burns victim, or a new heart can be transplanted into a patient with heart failure.

The procedure used is similar to that used to create Dolly the sheep, in that a human egg has its nucleus removed and the DNA from another human cell inserted into the egg and is then subjected to an electric shock. The resulting 'embryo' will develop stem cells (undifferentiated cells) that can be removed and grown *in vitro* into potentially any human cell, tissue or organ.

Therapeutic cloning by somatic cell nuclear transfer clearly offers exciting possibilities to improve human health and help cure debilitating diseases; however, at the same time it raises many ethical considerations. Many people argue that the created 'embryo' is a human life and if implanted into a female **surrogate** has the capacity to develop into a human being.

Human reproductive cloning

Reproductive cloning would involve making human clones, a process which has not yet been carried out, is illegal in many countries and is totally abhorrent to many people on a number of levels, through religious, cultural or personal beliefs. Some advocates for human cloning believe it would offer infertile couples the chance to have children, by creating a clone of either of themselves. The question remains, what relationship would a mother have with a clone of herself? Others argue that parents who have lost a child through death may wish the opportunity to clone their son or daughter.

Pet cloning

The first commercially cloned pet was a kitten cloned from a domestic cat in Texas, USA, in 2004, for a cost of around $50 000. The cloning of a dead pet has become a global commercial service, which is incredibly expensive as well as being controversial. Critics argue that it is unethical to clone dead pets, given the expense and the number of abandoned animals that could be given a good home instead. Others believe it is a step towards human reproductive cloning. On the other hand, advocates for pet cloning believe the techniques could be useful in preserving highly endangered animals on the brink of extinction.

Have your say!

1 What is your opinion about cloning animals?

2 Under what circumstances, if any, do you believe it is right to clone animals or plants?

3 If cloning a 'lost child' was permitted, would the parents be getting the same child back?

Case study: DNA and genetically modified organisms (GMO)

Medicine

Many important and life-saving medicines have been produced by genetically manipulating (changing) the DNA of one organism by inserting that of another.

Insulin production

Insulin, produced by the pancreas, is the hormone which helps control blood sugar levels. Diabetes sufferers cannot make their own insulin and previously they had to inject insulin from pigs. After the discovery of DNA, it was possible to identify the location of the gene coding for the protein insulin in a healthy individual and insert it into a bacterial cell which would multiply and grow to produce the protein in large quantities, in a process called genetic engineering.

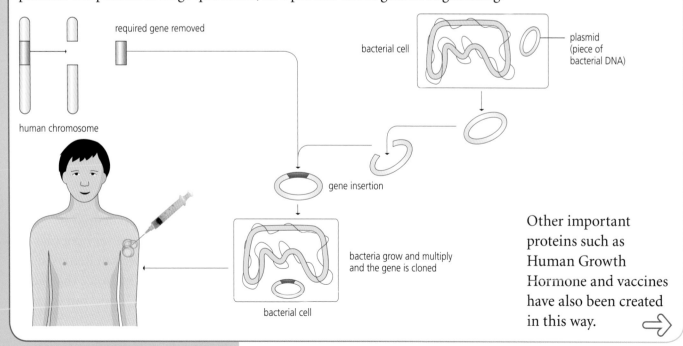

required gene removed

human chromosome

bacterial cell

plasmid (piece of bacterial DNA)

gene insertion

bacteria grow and multiply and the gene is cloned

bacterial cell

Other important proteins such as Human Growth Hormone and vaccines have also been created in this way.

Transgenic animals

Much research is being carried out to create a variety of **transgenic** animals that can produce proteins or substances useful to mankind.

Transgenic cattle

Dairy cattle can have a desired human gene inserted into them, in order for them to produce human proteins that can be collected from their milk and used to create medicines to treat a range of human conditions, such as blood clotting factors for **haemophilia**. Essentially these animals can be used as a factory for producing medicines for humans. There have even been dairy cattle that have had the human gene for producing human milk protein inserted into them, in order for them to produce human milk protein as opposed to cows' milk. This technology has been developed to help produce human milk on a large scale to help nourish starving or premature babies in developing countries.

Transgenic pigs

Transgenic pigs have been created to produce human organs for transplant e.g. heart valves.

'Glow in the dark' pigs were created in Taiwan several years ago by adding the DNA of jellyfish into pig embryos, which were then inserted into several surrogate sows. The resulting piglets were able to produce the fluorescent protein coded for in jellyfish DNA and as a result, glow in the dark.

Some transgenic pigs hold a potential solution to the shortage of organs for human transplantation. Pig organs have been used in human transplants for many years, however, the risk of rejection of the organ by the human immune system is very high and people with a transplanted organ must take drugs to suppress the immune system for the rest of their lives. By creating transgenic pigs, it would be possible to insert a gene into the DNA of a pig to produce a protein that helps protect the transplanted organ against the donor's immune system, reducing the likelihood of rejection. These transgenic pigs could be reared to provide humans with a constant source of organs for transplantation.

Transgenic mice and disease

Scientists are hoping to understand human disease through **stem cell** research of this kind. For example, some transgenic animals have been created as disease models, where they have had their DNA genetically changed to show symptoms of disease.

This enables scientists to develop potential treatments for the disease. Mice are very popular animals to use in this type of research. Removing genes from their DNA and breeding mice that lack certain genes created mice called 'knockout mice'.

Animals lacking certain genes may be unable to produce certain important proteins and this helps scientists understand the function of each gene. A mutant that carries a gene to encourage the development of certain human cancers has also been created and patented. It is called the Harvard mouse. It is hoped that by investigating the effects of certain drugs and treatments on these mice, a breakthrough in a cure or effective treatment for cancer can be discovered.

Have your say!

1 What is your opinion about using animals as 'medicine factories'?

2 How ethical is it to cause cancers in mice in order that scientists can study the disease in a laboratory?

3 How do you feel about breeding pigs only to harvest their organs for human transplantation?

4 'Exciting life-saving discoveries have been made through the use of animals in research.' To what extent do you agree or disagree with this statement?

5 If someone close to you developed a life-threatening illness and was offered a drug that had not been tested on animals and its safety was not fully understood, what would your opinion be of them taking this medication?

Case study: DNA and genetically modified foods (GM)

With the ever-increasing human population, it is estimated that there will be a global food shortage. In some drought-ridden areas of the world it is almost impossible to grow food crops, therefore scientists hope to introduce the gene for drought resistance into a crop plant's genome and grow these genetically modified plants in dry countries to provide the local people with a food source.

By inserting genes for resistance to disease and insect pests, a farmer can reduce the quantity of herbicides and pesticides sprayed on the crops, and thus reduce both cost and potential pollution problems. Strawberry plants have been genetically engineered to produce antifreeze, a chemical that helps them withstand frost damage, whereas other plants have had a gene inserted to help extend their shelf life. There appear to be many useful applications, however, many people find the idea of eating GM food totally unacceptable, and some pressure groups, such as GreenPeace, fear that cross-pollination between GM crops and wild plants will result in a decrease in biodiversity.

Have your say!

1 What is your opinion on eating plants that have had genes from another organism inserted into them?

2 It has been claimed that GM crops, modified to include disease resistance, can reduce the need for herbicides and other chemicals. Conduct a research project into this claim.

Case study: DNA and forensic science

There is no such thing as a 'perfect crime'! Fingerprints have been used since the nineteenth century to catch criminals. Tiny samples of saliva or hair contain enough DNA to link a suspect to the scene of the crime by making a **gene profile** (DNA fingerprint).

When a sample of DNA has been located at a crime scene, its genetic code is analysed in a laboratory to create a genetic profile, which is unique to that individual. Police scientists can then take and analyse DNA samples from suspects connected to the crime and compare the genetic code of the resulting DNA profiles to that found at the crime scene. This technology has proven to be invaluable in both eliminating suspects from crimes and proving the identity of criminals. This has allowed the police to stop investigating the people who have been eliminated and spend more time trying to catch the real criminals. DNA profiling has lead to many successful convictions.

Interestingly, the widespread use of DNA profiling has resulted in many criminals who are serving a jail sentence having been convicted on fingerprint evidence alone, appealing against their convictions. Stored critical evidence from the crime scene may contain or lack DNA samples that could either prove or disprove that the convict was indeed connected to that particular crime. The availability of post-conviction DNA analysis can offer some hope to convicts who have been found guilty of a crime of which they are innocent, and lead to their release from prison.

The opposite of this is also true. Some people acquitted from a trial many years ago, on the basis of other evidence, may now be shown to be connected to the crime following the advancement of DNA technology and analysis. However, in law a person acquitted from a trial cannot be retried for the same crime.

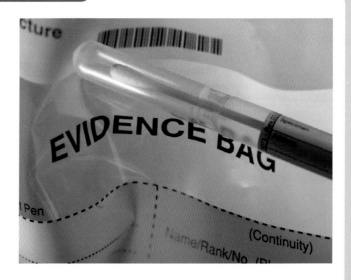

Advancement in DNA technology has resulted in people now being convicted of crimes that were committed many, many years ago. In some cases, the people who were prime suspects many years ago, but were not tried because of a lack of evidence, can now be successfully convicted on the basis of re-examining evidence and analysing DNA.

Have your say!

1 Should the law be changed to allow people to be retried when new evidence has been located?

2 If the law was to be changed and a person could be tried twice, what confidence would people have in our legal and policing system in the UK?

3 Do you think that DNA evidence alone should be enough to convict someone of a crime?

4 Where do you see the strengths and weaknesses of DNA evidence in criminal trials?

5 Should a national database of everyone's DNA be held by the government?

Case study: DNA history, genealogy, databases and citizenship

It is possible to trace family trees and confirm the identity of your ancestors and even your parents by having your DNA analysed. DNA profiling is often used for paternity tests, to prove or disprove if an alleged father is the biological father of a child. It can also confirm if twins are identical or non-identical, as well as whether siblings (brothers and sisters) are biological siblings.

Some people trace their family histories to look for **inherited** diseases. Before trying for a baby many couples who are concerned that they may carry the gene causing genetic diseases such as Tay-Sachs or Cystic Fibrosis have their DNA analysed to assess the risk of having a child with the disease. As a result some couples make what must be a difficult decision, not to have children.

If you suspected you carried the gene for a genetic disease, would you choose to have your DNA analysed to find out?

DNA profiling – identification of individuals

DNA profiling plays a very important role in identifying the remains of people killed after catastrophes, wars or natural disasters such as tsunamis and earthquakes. In these situations it can be very difficult to identify individuals from their appearance or dental records. Since no two people, apart from identical twins, have the same DNA, it is possible to establish the identity of a person by taking a sample of their DNA from a skin or hair sample. This method can help make positive identifications of individuals, when other methods are not possible.

DNA profiling and the workplace

This may sound a little like something out of a science fiction or futuristic novel, but some companies offer DNA profiling to their staff members. A simple mouth swab, containing DNA from saliva provides DNA profiles of individual staff members, which can be held on record. This would offer the company a DNA profile or genetic blueprint for every member of staff.

Have your say!

1　What is your opinion? Do you feel this is acceptable or do you feel this compromises a person's human or civil liberties?

2　Why do you think some companies would want to profile their employees' DNA?

3　How would you feel if your school wanted to take a sample of your DNA to add to their genetic profile of pupils?

4　Can you think of any organisations where this level of unique identification would be required or justified?

5　Could this genetic information be used to discriminate against members of staff in a company or organisation?

GLOSSARY

The base sequence the arrangement of chemical bases inside DNA that provides the genetic code for an individual

Chromosome structures, visible during cell division, that are made of DNA and protein

Chromosome complement the number of chromosomes inside a species

Cloning making an exact genetic copy of an individual

Cystic Fibrosis an inherited disease

Deoxyribose the sugar that is found in DNA

DNA the chemical that transfers genetic information between living things

DNA fingerprinting or **DNA profiling** process for identifying an individual on the basis of the sequence in their DNA

DNA replication process of copying DNA that takes place when cells divide

Electrophoresis scientific technique that is used to separate electrically charged materials

Forensic using science for legal purposes

Gene profile the products of a genetic profile/fingerprint

Gene therapy using genetic engineering to transplant genes into cells to cure inherited disease

Genetic code the precise sequence of chemical bases within individual DNA

Genetically modified organism an organism that has been produced using genetic engineering to transplant genes into the organism

Haemophilia an inherited disease

Helix a spiral

In vitro a biological experiment that takes place in a container

Mutate a chemical change in DNA that results in different appearance or properties

Nobel Prize annual award for the most outstanding global contribution to physics, chemistry, physiology and medicine

Nucleotide bases four chemicals – abbreviated to A, T, G and C – that make up the genetic code

Restriction enzyme an enzyme that is used to cut DNA in small pieces when making a genetic profile

Sibling brother or sister

Stem cell a cell that is capable of reproducing and specialising in a number of different ways

Surrogate substitute

Transgenic living things that include genes from another species

Tumour a mass of uncontrolled cell growth

X-ray diffraction experimental technique used to discover the arrangement of atoms inside chemicals

Curriculum for Excellence mapping grid

Curriculum for Excellence Science Level 3 Experiences and Outcomes		Chapter	1	2	3	4	5	6	7	8	9	10	11	12	13
Planet Earth		SCN 3-01a	■												
		SCN 3-02a		■											
		SCN 3-03a			■										
		SCN 3-04a													
		SCN 3-04b													
		SCN 3-05a													
		SCN 3-05b				■									
		SCN 3-06a				■									
Forces, Electricity and Waves		SCN 3-07a							■						
		SCN 3-08a					■								
		SCN 3-09a													
		SCN 3-10a							■						
		SCN 3-11a													
		SCN 3-11b						■							
Biological Systems		SCN 3-12a							■						
		SCN 3-12b								■					
		SCN 3-13a									■				
		SCN 3-13b										■			
		SCN 3-13c											■		
		SCN 3-14a												■	
		SCN 3-14b													■
Materials		SCN 3-15a													
		SCN 3-15b													
		SCN 3-16a													
		SCN 3-16b													
		SCN 3-17a	■												
		SCN 3-17b		■											
		SCN 3-18a													
		SCN 3-19a													
		SCN 3-19b													

The Publishers would like to thank the following for permission to reproduce copyright material:

Photo credits
p.7 (bottom from left) © KBImages/Alamy, © Martin Hughes-Jones/Alamy, © WILDLIFE GmbH/Alamy, © Paul Hebditch/Alamy; p.8 (top from left) © Douglas Fisher/Alamy, © Tony Rolls/Alamy, © Kevin Schafer/CORBIS; p.11 (bottom left) © FORGET Patrick/SAGAPHOTO.COM/Alamy; p.12 (top left) PH. PLAILLY/EURELIOS/SCIENCE PHOTO LIBRARY, (top right) © SINCLAIR STAMMERS/SCIENCE PHOTO LIBRARY; p.14 (right) © Gordon Buchanan; p.17 (top) © Imagestate Media, (middle) © David Whitaker/Alamy, (bottom left) Albaimages/Alamy, (bottom right) BOB GIBBONS/SCIENCE PHOTO LIBRARY; p.20 (bottom) © mike lane/Alamy; p.21 (top left) © WK Photos/Alamy, (top right) © Andrew Lambert Photography/Science Photo Library; p.26 © Stockbyte/Photolibrary Group Ltd; p.27 © Hamilton Grammar School; p.32 (top right) © Imagestate Media, (middle right) © Photodisc/Getty Images; p.33 (top right) © tom carter/Alamy, (bottom left) © Glenn Frank/iStockphoto.com; p.35 (top) © William Gottlieb/CORBIS, (bottom left) © Karen Struthers - Fotolia.com, (bottom middle) © Photolibrary.Com, (bottom right) © Dušan Zidar - Fotolia.com; p.36 © LWA-Dann Tardif/Corbis; p.37 © NIGEL CATTLIN/SCIENCE PHOTO LIBRARY; p.38 (top left) © Design Pics Inc. - RM Content/Alamy, (bottom left) Derek Croucher/Getty Images, (top right) © BSIP MARTIN PL./SCIENCE PHOTO LIBRARY, (bottom right) © Photodisc/Photolibrary Group Ltd; p.39 (top) JOHN DEVRIES/SCIENCE PHOTO LIBRARY, (bottom) © Nigel Cattlin/Visuals Unlimited/Corbis; p.40 (left) © Barrett & MacKay/Photolibrary, (right) © Imagestate Media; p.41 © Vincent MacNamara/Alamy; p.42 © Mary H. Swift/Alamy; p.45 NASA Goddard Space Flight Center (NASA-GSFC); p.48 ©Stockbyte/Photolibrary Group Ltd; p.50 NASA Marshall Space Flight Center (NASA-MSFC); p.51 (top) © Johner Images/Alamy, (bottom left) NASA/SCIENCE PHOTO LIBRARY, (bottom right) © Reuters/CORBIS; p.52 (top) © Corbis, (bottom left) SCIENCE SOURCE/SCIENCE PHOTO LIBRARY, (bottom right) AFP/Getty Images; p.53 (left) NASA/SCIENCE PHOTO LIBRARY, (right) © Galaxy Picture Library; p.55 (top left) NASA/SCIENCE PHOTO LIBRARY, (bottom left) © NASA/Reuters/Corbis, (top right) RIA NOVOSTI/SCIENCE PHOTO LIBRARY, (bottom right) NASA/SCIENCE PHOTO LIBRARY; p.56 (top) RIA NOVOSTI/SCIENCE PHOTO LIBRARY, (middle left) NASA/SCIENCE PHOTO LIBRARY, (middle right) Bloomberg via Getty Images, (bottom left) © Peter Arnold, Inc./Alamy, (bottom right) NASA/SCIENCE PHOTO LIBRARY; p.57 © NASA; p.58 A. DOWSETT, HEALTH PROTECTION AGENCY/SCIENCE PHOTO LIBRARY; p.61 (top left) © Photodisc/Getty Images, (bottom right) DR KEITH WHEELER/SCIENCE PHOTO LIBRARY; p.62 (middle left) © imagebroker/Alamy, (middle right) PATRICK LANDMANN/SCIENCE PHOTO LIBRARY, (bottom) ©JAN HINSCH/SCIENCE PHOTO LIBRARY; p.63 (top) © Trevor Smith/Alamy, (bottom) © Enigma/Alamy; p.64 (top) © Glenn Tattersall/Brock University, (bottom left) MILpictures by Tom Weber/Getty Images, (bottom right) EDWARD KINSMAN/SCIENCE PHOTO LIBRARY; p.65 (top) SCIENCE PHOTO LIBRARY; p.66 (top right) SOVEREIGN, ISM/SCIENCE PHOTO LIBRARY, (top left) BJORN RORSLETT/SCIENCE PHOTO LIBRARY, (bottom left) © Jochen Tack/Alamy, (bottom right) ©Photodisc/Getty Images; p.67 (top) © Mary Turner/Rex Features, (middle) © Stockbyte/Getty Images, (bottom) OHIO-NUCLEAR CORPORATION/SCIENCE PHOTO, LIBRARY; p.70 (left) ©Paul Broadbent/Alamy; p.73 GEORGE MUSIL, VISUALS UNLIMITED/SCIENCE PHOTO LIBRARY; p.74 © Klaas Lingbeek- van Kranen/iStockphoto; p.78 (top left) © PLATRIEZ PLATRIEZ/Photolibrary, (bottom left) © Stockbyte/Getty Images, (right) © Sang Il Park and Jessica K. Hodgins; p.79 PHILIPPE PSAILA/SCIENCE PHOTO LIBRARY; p.80 (left) From www.lateralscience.co.uk, (right) © Visuals Unlimited/Corbis; p.81 (left) RICCARDO CASSIANI-INGONI/SCIENCE PHOTO LIBRARY, (right) ©Photodisc/Getty Images; p.84 (top left) © UNESCO, (top right) © World Health Organisation (WHO), (bottom) ©JIM VARNEY/SCIENCE PHOTO LIBRARY; p.86 (top left) L Steinmark/Getty Images, (bottom left) DR P. MARAZZI/SCIENCE PHOTO LIBRARY, (top right) © Blend Images/Alamy; p.87 (top) © ImageState/Alamy, (bottom) © Photodisc/Getty Images; p.88 (top) © Stockbyte/Alamy, (bottom) © imagebroker/Alamy; p.89 (left) MARTYN F. CHILLMAID/SCIENCE PHOTO LIBRARY, (right) © Steve Morgan/Alamy; p.90 (top left) P. SAADA/EURELIOS/SCIENCE PHOTO LIBRARY, (bottom left) © imagebroker/Alamy, (right) © Trinity Mirror/Mirrorpix/Alamy; p.92 AJ PHOTO/SCIENCE PHOTO LIBRARY;

p.94 © NASA Marshall Space Flight Center (NASA-MSFC); p.96 (top left) ERIC GRAVE/SCIENCE PHOTO LIBRARY, (top right) STEVE GSCHMEISSNER/SCIENCE PHOTO LIBRARY, (bottom) ROLAND BIRKE/PETER ARNOLD INC./SCIENCE PHOTO LIBRARY; p.97 (right) ©PHOTOTAKE Inc./Alamy; p.98 (left) DAVID MCCARTHY/SCIENCE PHOTO LIBRARY; p.103 (left) ©Photodisc/Getty Images, (top right) STEVE ALLEN/SCIENCE PHOTO LIBRARY, (bottom right) DR KARI LOUNATMAA/SCIENCE PHOTO LIBRARY; p.106 (top left) © EYE OF SCIENCE/SCIENCE PHOTO LIBRARY, (top right, clockwise from top left) JAN HINSCH/SCIENCE PHOTO LIBRARY, DR. PETER SIVER, VISUALS UNLIMITED/SCIENCE PHOTO LIBRARY, CDC/SCIENCE PHOTO LIBRARY, EYE OF SCIENCE/SCIENCE PHOTO LIBRARY (bottom right) © Seth Resnick/Science Faction/Corbis; p.107 (left) © Envision/Corbis, (centre) © Gerrit Buntrock/Photolibrary, (right) ©PHOTOTAKE Inc./Alamy; p.108 (left) ©Steven May/Alamy, (right) HUGH SPENCER/SCIENCE PHOTO LIBRARY; p.109 (top left) SCIENCE VU , VISUALS UNLIMITED/SCIENCE PHOTO LIBRARY, (bottom left) © 2005 Agarwal et al; licensee BioMed Central Ltd., (top right) NASA/GSFC/SCIENCE PHOTO LIBRARY, (bottom right) Courtesy of Wikipedia Commons; p.110 (top left) SCIENCE PHOTO LIBRARY, (bottom left) DR P. MARAZZI/SCIENCE PHOTO LIBRARY, (right) DAVID MACK/SCIENCE PHOTO LIBRARY; p.111 (top left) © Photodisc/Getty Images, (bottom left) © Stockbyte/Getty Images, (right) © ALAN OLIVER/Alamy; p.112 (left) SSPL via Getty Images, (top right) © Bon Appetit/Alamy, (bottom right) © STEVE LINDRIDGE/Alamy; p.113 (left) DR. TERRY BEVERIDGE, VISUALS UNLIMITED/SCIENCE PHOTO LIBRARY; p.114 (middle) © fotoshoot/Alamy, (bottom) SCIENCE SOURCE/SCIENCE PHOTO LIBRARY; p.115 (left) © Corbis Premium RF/Alamy, (top right) © uli nusko/Alamy, (bottom right) © Brawdahlia on Flickr.com; p.120 © Suzanne Tucker/iStockphoto; p.125 © World History Archive/Alamy; p.128 BSIP, LAURENT/SCIENCE PHOTO LIBRARY; p.131 (left) © Homer Sykes Archive/Alamy, (top right) FRANCIS LEROY, BIOCOSMOS/SCIENCE PHOTO LIBRARY, (bottom right) CC STUDIO/SCIENCE PHOTO LIBRARY; p.132 (top) PROFESSORS P.M. MOTTA & J. VAN BLERKOM/SCIENCE PHOTO LIBRARY, (bottom) PROF. P. MOTTA/DEPT. OF ANATOMY/UNIVERSITY "LA SAPIENZA", ROME/SCIENCE PHOTO LIBRARY; p.133 (top) D. PHILLIPS/SCIENCE PHOTO LIBRARY, (bottom) © Imagestate Media; p.134 (top) © Henrik Jonsson/iStockphoto, (middle) PASCAL GOETGHELUCK/SCIENCE PHOTO LIBRARY, (bottom) © MedicalRF.com/Alamy; p.135 (top) EDELMANN/SCIENCE PHOTO LIBRARY, (bottom) © Imagestate Media; p.137 © Martin Shields/Alamy; p.138 (left) © Imagestate Media, (right) © Bubbles Photolibrary/Alamy; p.139 ZEPHYR/SCIENCE PHOTO LIBRARY; p.140 Getty Images; p.141 (top) © vario images GmbH & Co.KG/Alamy, (bottom left) CNRI/SCIENCE PHOTO LIBRARY, (bottom right) © Chad Ehlers/Alamy; p.142 (from top) © Sally and Richard Greenhill/Alamy, MOREDUN ANIMAL HEALTH LTD/SCIENCE PHOTO LIBRARY, © Crown Copyright, PRINCESS MARGARET ROSE ORTHOPAEDIC HOSPITAL/SCIENCE PHOTO LIBRARY; p.143 (top) © RIA NOVOSTI/SCIENCE PHOTO LIBRARY, (bottom) © lawrence white/Alamy; p.144 (left) © IVF Scotland, (top right) MAURO FERMARIELLO/SCIENCE PHOTO LIBRARY, (bottom right) DR NAJEEB LAYYOUS/SCIENCE PHOTO LIBRARY; p.147 (top) © Trinity Mirror/Mirrorpix/Alamy; p.148 © Corbis Premium RF/Alamy; p.149 SCIENCE PHOTO LIBRARY; p.151 (left) © MAURO FERMARIELLO/SCIENCE PHOTO LIBRARY; p.152 DR GOPAL MURTI/SCIENCE PHOTO LIBRARY; p.154 (top) © Ramiro Alberio/University of Nottingham, (bottom) © Neil Setchfield/Alamy; p.156 (right) © Simon Lin/AP/Press Association Images; p.157 ADRIAN THOMAS/SCIENCE PHOTO LIBRARY; p.158 ©TEK IMAGE/SCIENCE PHOTO LIBRARY.
p.7 (top left and right), p.8 (top and bottom right), p.9, p.10, p.11 (bottom right), p.13 (all), p.15, p.16, p.19 (all), p.20 (top), p.21 (bottom left and right), p.22 (all), p.30, p.32 (bottom left and right), p.33 (top left), p.62 (top), p.85, p.97 (left), p.98 (right), p.101, p.106 (bottom left), p.113 (right), p.114 (top), p.116 (all), p.147 (bottom all), p.151 (right) © Nicky Souter; p.14 (left), p.18, p.32 (top right),p.65 (bottom all), p.70 (bottom all), p.87 (middle), p.91, p.102, p.156 (left) © Hodder Gibson; p.6, p.25, p.34, p.44, p.105 © Digital Stock; p.54 and p.59 © MEDICAL RF.COM/SCIENCE PHOTO LIBRARY; p.69, p.82, p.93, p.118, p.130, p.146 © Photodisc/Getty Images.

Every effort has been made to trace all copyright holders, but if any have been inadvertently overlooked the Publishers will be pleased to make the necessary arrangements at the first opportunity.